MESSAGES OF INSPIRATION

Volume II

Messages to Inspire, Uplift, Encourage, and Strengthen the Body of Christ

Dr. J. L. Williams

Copyright © 2013 by Dr. J. L. Williams

Messages of Inspiration
Volume II
by Dr. J. L. Williams

Printed in the United States of America

ISBN 9781626970731

All rights reserved solely by the author. The author guarantees all contents are original and do not infringe upon the legal rights of any other person or work. No part of this book may be reproduced in any form without the permission of the author. The views expressed in this book are not necessarily those of the publisher.

Unless otherwise indicated, Bible quotations are taken from King James Version of the Bible.

Scripture marked NKJV is taken from the New King James Version®. Copyright © 1982 by Thomas Nelson, Inc. Used by permission. All rights reserved.

www.xulonpress.com

Preface

**Messages of Inspiration
Volume II**

These are messages to inspire your faith—faith to believe the impossible and expect the miraculous in your life—a life that God has diligently and thoughtfully planned out in time.

These are messages to inspire you to look more closely, to be drawn more deeply, and to go far beyond your expectations; messages to experience the presence of God in a glorious way, never before imagined.

Dedication

This book is dedicated to my three grandchildren, Asiah, Darius, and Autumn, who are truly gifts from above. They are precious and priceless, and I love them dearly. They are a reminder of how great and awesome is the God that I serve.

To my pastor, Dr. LeRoy Howard, and to the first lady, Sister Hattie P. Howard. To the New Zion Missionary Baptist Church family of Clearwater, Florida, thank you for all your prayers, your presence, and your support throughout this project and beyond. Dr. Howard, you've inspired the Jabez in me to grow and my territories to expand. I consider it not only a blessing, but also a privilege to know you, as an excellent teacher, and a kind and encouraging friend. Thank you for believing in me. May God's blessings continue to pour out on you.

Table of Contents

Message #1	Praise the Lord, for He Is Worthy to Be Praised!	11
Message #2	The God That Does Not Change	15
Message #3	God's Resurrection Power	17
Message #4	Who Is This Jesus?	21
Message #5	Trust in the Lord	27
Message #6	Let No Man Despise Your Youth	29
Message #7	What Is His Name?	33
Message #8	More Than a Conqueror	39
Message #9	Young People, God Wants You to Be an Eagle	43
Message #10	Young People, Everything Is Going to Be All Right	47
Message #11	Hope Beyond This Life	55
Message #12	The Blood of Jesus	61
Message #13	Heaven or Hell: The Choice Is Yours	67
Message #14	It's Time for the Redeemed of the Lord to Say So	71
Message #15	God's Detergent	77
Message #16	God Is Still God	85
Message #17	God Didn't Bring Us This Far to Leave Us	89

Message #1

Praise the Lord, for He Is Worthy to Be Praised!

Scripture Text: 1 Peter 2:9, Psalm 150:6

The Bible verse 1 Peter 2:9 not only appoints praise, but also represents a basic revelation of the Bible. This verse emphasizes that God wants people who will walk with Him in prayer, march with Him in praise, thank and worship Him. Note the progression in Peter's description of the people of the new covenant (four points):

1. We are a *chosen generation*. These chosen people started with Jesus's choice of twelve individuals, who grew to a following of one hundred twenty people and later thousands at Pentecost. We are a part of this continually expanding generation "chosen" when we receive Christ.

2. We are a *royal priesthood*. Under the old covenant, the priesthood and royalty were separated. We are now in the person of our Lord—all kings and priests to His God (Revelation 1:6). We are a *worshipping host and a kingly band*, prepared for walking with Him in the light or warring beside Him against the hosts of darkness.

3. We are a *"holy nation"* composed of Jews and Gentiles—of one blood, from everything , every nation under heaven.

4. We are His *"special"* people. God's intention from the time of Abraham has been to call forth a people with a special mission—to proclaim His praise and to propagate His blessing throughout the earth (Hebrews 13:10-15; Genesis 29:35).

Psalm 150:6 states: "Let everything that hath breath praise the Lord. Praise ye the Lord." We are first told in this verse who is to worship: *everything that breathes*. Then it closes by restating the object of worship—*the Lord*. The final commentary reveals that every living thing should praise the Lord! In case one person feels less than inclined to praise Him, the instruction is clear: *If you have God's gift of life and breath, you should praise Him! Hallelujah!*

When you begin to bless and praise the Lord, the Lord listens and says, "Listen to My people down there praising and blessing Me and thanking Me for My mighty exploits!" He tells the angels to run to their dispatch, make the crooked way straight; uplift the valley, silence the mouths of accusers, hold back the lions, open the windows of heaven and pour out on us a blessing we cannot contain. While we praise him, he continues to tell us, "Those are My children. Bind the powers of darkness, bind the powers of principalities, hold the demons back and bless them with My power, for the spirit of praise and thanksgiving has released the anointing of God in their lives." Give Him praise!

I don't know about you, but I'm glad that my sins are gone. If you are washed in the blood of the Lamb, then you have a right to rejoice. You have a right to praise *God*, because your name is written down in the Lamb's book of life! *You* were born again to praise *God*. You should come to church shouting, "Glory!" "Hallelujah!" "Glory to God!" "Thank You, Jesus!" "My God, I'm saved! I'm on my way to heaven! I've got power over the devil. God has delivered me out of the hands of the enemy! Thank God I'm His child, and I'm going to rejoice!" Go ahead and rejoice! The apostle Paul tells the church at Philippi to rejoice. I say, "Always!" And again I say, "Rejoice!"

The psalmist David said, "I'm going to praise Him in the morning! I'm going to praise Him at the noonday hour! I'm going to praise Him when the sun goes down!" (Psalm 113:3). Then David said, "That's not enough. I'm going to write a new psalm. I'm going to praise Him on my early rising! I'm going to praise Him when I go out! I'm going to praise Him during the lunch break! I'm going to praise Him in the afternoon! I'm going to praise Him on the way home! I'm going to praise Him at the supper hour! And before I go to bed, I'm going to praise Him! If I can't sleep, I'll get up and praise the Lord!" (Psalm 63:1,6).

David said, "That's still not enough! I'm going to write a new psalm!" (Psalm 34:1). "His praise, His praise shall continually be in my mouth!" Go ahead and praise Him! Praise Him! He makes my feet run like hinds' feet! Jesus said, "I'll give you joy that no man can give you, and I'll give you joy that no man can take away from you!" Talking about joy! The joy of the Lord! The joy of the Lord! The joy of the Lord is your strength! Praise the Lord, Church! Praise the Lord, Church! For He is worthy, worthy, worthy to be praised!

Message #2

The God That Does Not Change

Scripture Text: Hebrews 13:8

Definition of change: To cause to be different, to alter, or to transform.

When we read the Scripture text, "Jesus Christ is the same yesterday, and today, and forever," what is it telling us? It is the doctrine of immutability, which means that *God Almighty* has never, can never, and will never change! He is, by His very nature, unchangeable!

This means that He is as powerful as ever; He is as loving, as merciful, as full of grace, as holy, and as much in control as He has ever been. He is still *God*, and He will always be *God*! He is absolutely unchangeable. Jesus has all power in heaven and earth, and nothing can change this fact!

He has creative power – This is the same power that is working in and around us. That is why we can say with all assurance of heart, that *"Jesus is able!"*

He has redemptive power – Jesus is the Author and Finisher of our faith. That is, He paid the price and He is the only one in whom salvation can be found!

He has protective power – Jesus is still the Good Shepherd, and He will care for the sheep until they all arrive safely home!

He is also a *God* that keeps His promises – He has promised to save us. The promise is clear. When a lost sinner comes to Jesus by faith, he or she is saved by grace and prepared for heaven. This is a promise that will never change.

He has promised to supply us – Again, the promise is clear. *God* will take care of you! And He will supply your needs according to His riches in glory by Christ Jesus!

He has promised to satisfy us – When Jesus met the woman at the well, He promised her a drink of living water that would eternally satisfy her thirsty soul!

He has promised to secure us – There is no doctrine more precious to the saints of God than the doctrine of our eternal security in the Lord Jesus Christ, because in salvation, God justifies the sinner and declares us righteous, putting away all our sins—past, present, and future.

He has promised to sustain us – God has promised to give us grace along the way. He may not remove the burden, but He will give you grace to bear the burden, for He is—"A burden-bearer and a heavy-load sharer!"

We are living in changing times! We are living in extraordinary times! We are living in uncertain times! We are living in a time where the rubber is meeting the road! We are living in a time where businesses that have had success for twenty, thirty, forty, fifty, or one hundred or more years have closed their doors for good. Major corporations have changed their ways and policies, but our Lord Jesus Christ is faithful. He does not change!

The seasons change! The law changes! Time changes! People change! Finances change! The way society thinks may change! But Jesus Christ does not change! He's the same yesterday, and today, and forever! His mercy, His love, His kindness, His grace does not change! Your job may change and relocate! Your job classification may change! Your friends may change! But Jesus never changes! He is the same yesterday, and today, and forever!

Can I get a witness? I need somebody to give Him praise and bless His name! Has Jesus been good to you? Has He blessed your life? Has He made a way for you? If He has been good to you, raise your hands and shout, "Yes!" Shout, "Yes!" Shout, "Yes!"

Message #3

God's Resurrection Power

Scripture Text: St. Matthew 28:5-6

This is the story of the resurrection of Jesus. When the two Marys went to the sepulcher—Mary Magdalene and the other Mary, who was the mother of James and Joses, and the mother of Zebedee's children—they were met by an angel who told them that Jesus had risen.

We are on the premise of one of the most celebrated Christian holidays there is: Resurrection Sunday! Out of all the world's religions, one of the doctrines that separates Christianity from the others is the Resurrection. It has always been a cardinal article of faith in the Christian Church. If you were to go to the graves of Mohammed, Buddha, and the like, and unearth their graves, their remains would still be there. But our Lord and Savior, Jesus Christ, is not in His tomb, because He arose from the grave, just as He said He would! And He backs it up when He showed Himself alive to His apostles, after His passion, by many infallible proofs (Acts 1:3).

Resurrection Sunday is what the Christian faith is based upon, and I am here to declare unto you that God's resurrection power is still working mightily in the earth today! His power is still resurrecting broken lives and shattered dreams! His power is still resurrecting souls from the kingdom of darkness, into the kingdom of light! His power is still resurrecting lives that were shackled under the bondage of sin! His power is still resurrecting the hearts and minds of people all over the world, because He is a heart fixer and a mind regulator! His power is still resurrecting in the hearts of His children. In St. John chapter 11 and verse 25, Jesus told Martha that, "I am the resurrection and the life."

In conclusion, over two thousand years ago, on a hill called Golgotha, on a Friday, our Lord was crucified. After the crucifixion, things began to happen. From the sixth to the ninth hour, darkness covered the whole earth, the sun was darkened, and the veil of the temple was torn from top to bottom. The earth did quake, and the graves were opened, and many of the bodies of the saints which slept, arose.

After Jesus was declared dead, He was taken down from the cross and was buried in a borrowed tomb. The reason the tomb was borrowed was because it was only temporary, because early, early on Sunday morning, He rose with all power in heaven and in earth in His hands! And because of the resurrecting power of Jesus, we all can shout the victory! Can I get a witness of God's resurrection power? If you were dead in your sins, and now you have been made alive by God's resurrection power, will you help me praise Him? Glorify Him!

Some of you received God's resurrection power on a Sunday, some on a Monday, some on a Tuesday, some on a Wednesday, some on a Thursday, some on a Friday, and some on a Saturday. Some of you received God's resurrection power early in the morning; some may have received it in the noon hour; some may have received it in the afternoon; some may have received it in the evening; and some may have received it in the midnight hour! But whenever you received God's resurrection power, you should be thankful; you should be praising Him; you should be glorifying Him and blessing Him!

Somebody in here should say like old doubting Thomas, "My Lord and my God!" If He is your Lord and your God, come on, somebody; help me praise Him! I don't know about you, but I am glad for God's resurrection power! If you are glad for God's resurrection power, shout, "Yes!" Shout, "Yes!" Shout, "Yes!"

Introduction

Galatians 1:4 – Who gave Himself for our sins, that He might deliver us from this present evil age, according to the will of our God and Father.

Paul the apostle summarizes the epistle by declaring the fact, the purpose, and the ground of redemption in Christ. Scripture divides history into two ages: this present age, dominated by Satan; and, "the age to come," inaugurated by Jesus. Since the present age has not yet passed away, the two ages are currently running on parallel courses. Jesus came to rescue us from the dominion of the old age, and to transfer us into life in the age to come.

1 Timothy 2:6 – Who gave Himself a ransom for all, to be testified in due time.

Jesus became a ransom for all mankind. Now a ransom is money paid or demanded for the release of a person held captive. However, it cost more than shining silver, or yellow gold, to pay our ransom for our sins. It took the precious, holy, spotless blood of our Lord Jesus Christ.

2 Timothy 1:9 – Who has saved us and called us with a holy calling, not according to our works, but according to His own purpose and grace, which was given to us in Christ Jesus before time began.

Salvation is entirely a matter of God's purpose and grace, apart from human works. Grace is not only the unmerited favor of God, but grace is also enabling power, it is divine ability, it is supernatural force that flows into your life, into your circumstance, into your situation, empowering you to do what you could not do, to receive what you could not receive, and to be what you could not be before you received that grace. If you noticed, the first word of each of the Scripture passages read today began with the pronoun "who." A pronoun is simply a word used as a substitute for a noun, words as *he, she,* or *it*.

Message #4

Who Is This Jesus?

Scripture Text: Galatians 1:4, 1 Timothy 2:6, 2 Timothy 1:9

In English composition, in order to get a complete story, you must ask the important six questions, the five "Ws" and the "H": Who, What, When, Where, Why, and the "H," How. I believe America is asking some of those questions today, regarding the war on terrorism. Example: Who are the terrorists? What do they want? When are they planning to strike the United States? Why do they want to terrorize the United States? Where will these terrorists strike next? And of course the "H," How are they going to strike?

When the company you work for is changing bosses, normally the employees ask the question: Who is going to be our new boss? Or if you are in school and you are told that a new principal or teacher or coach is coming to your school, the normal, appropriate question is: "Who" will be our new principal, teacher, or coach?

So today we are going to deal with the "W" entitled "Who." The title of this message is, "Who Is This Jesus?" Who is this Jesus? So let me tell you a little bit about who this Jesus is. He was God in the flesh, who came down to earth on a mission. And that mission was to save mankind from their sins. But before He could leave His heavenly throne, He had to take off some things. He had to take off His glory. He had to take off His omniscience. He had to take off His omnipresence. He had to take off His omnipotence. Then He had to come through forty-two generations.

He then had to be born of a virgin girl named Mary. He was born in a manger in Bethlehem because there was no more room in the inn. He lived on this earth for thirty-three years, and in those thirty-three years, He lived a sinless, perfect, holy life. He healed the sick, raised the dead, brought peace out of chaos, cleansed the lepers, opened blind eyes, made the dumb to speak, fed the multitudes with fish and bread, and then one Friday, over two thousand years ago, He was crucified on a cross—not for any crime that He had committed—but He became the sacrificial lamb for you and me, and for the sins of the world!

He was buried in a borrowed tomb. But on the third day, early, early, early, before the sun got up; early, early, early, before the roosters could crow; He rose from the grave with all power in His hands! And He lives forevermore! Who is this Jesus? He is:

- **A** – The Absolute Answer
- **B** – A Bondage Breaker
- **C** – The Compassionate Captain
- **D** – Devil Destroyer
- **E** – The Everlasting Emmanuel
- **F** – The Faithful Father
- **G** – The Gracious Giver
- **H** – Heaven's Hero
- **I** – The Immortal Intercessor
- **J** – Jehovah Jireh
- **K** – King of Kings
- **L** – Lord of Life
- **M** – Man's Mediator
- **N** – Noah's Navigator
- **O** – The Oasis in Dry Places
- **P** – Paul's Peace
- **Q** – Quickening Power
- **R** – The Refuge for Souls
- **S** – The Sacrificial Savior
- **T** – The Treasure of Heaven
- **U** – The Unconditional Lover
- **V** – The Victorious One
- **W** – Worthy of All Praise
- **X** – The Executor of Justice

Y – Yeshua HaMashiach
Z – Zechariah's Visions

Who Is This Jesus? He Is:

Elohim – The God who creates.
Jehovah – The God of life and eternity, who reveals Himself to us in a personal way.
El Shaddai – The all-sufficient God.
Adonai – He is the Master and we are His purchased possession.
Jehovah Jireh – The God who will provide.
Jehovah M'Kaddesh – The Lord my sanctifier; the One who sets me apart.
Jehovah Nissi – The Lord is my banner of victory.
Jehovah Rophe – The Lord who heals.
Jehovah Shalom – The Lord who is my peace.
Jehovah Tsidkenu – The Lord our righteousness.
Jehovah Rohi – The Lord my shepherd.
Jehovah Shammah – The Lord is present.
El Elyon – The most-high God.
Jehovah Tsebaoth – The Lord of Hosts.
Jehovah Makkeh – The Lord our smiter. His purpose is to mold us and shape us into smooth, lively stones.
Jehovah Gmolah – The Lord of recompenses.
Jehovah Elohay – The Lord my God.
El-Elohe-Israel – The Lord God of Israel.
Jehovah Eloheenu – The Lord our God.

Who Is This Jesus?

Some say He is a good man.
Some say He is a prophet.
Some say He is a fairy tale character, and does not exist.

But I tell you, He is more than a good man; He is more than just a prophet; and He does really exist. He is the Creator of all things; He is the Prince of Peace; He is the Almighty God; He is the Immortal, Invincible, Omnipresent One; the One who rules and reigns with all power.

In our court system today, when we have a criminal trial, there are several people who play a key role in the process. We have to have a judge, a prosecuting attorney, a defense attorney, a court reporter, a bailiff, the accused, the jury, and witnesses. Some witnesses will be testifying for the defense, and some will be testifying for the prosecution. Witnesses are a valuable part of any court case. The Bible tells me in 2 Corinthians chapter 13 and verse 1, it says: "By the mouth of two or three witnesses every word shall be established." So today I brought along with me a few witnesses to testify of who this Jesus is.

To Ezra: He was "Help."
To Nehemiah: He was "The Consoling Jehovah."
To Job: He was "The Hedge of Protection."
To Hosea: He was "Redeeming Love."
To Joel: He was "Jehovah is God."
To Amos: He was "A Burden Bearer."
To Obadiah: He was "The Servant of the Lord."
To Jonah: He was "God's Mercy."
To Micah: He was "Who is like the Lord."
To Nahum: He was "Compassionate."
To Habakkuk: He was "The Just Shall Live by Faith."
To Zephaniah: He was "The Lord Who Hides or Protects."
To Haggai: He was "The Rebuilder of the Temple."
To Zechariah: He was "Yahweh Remembers."
To Malachi: He was "My Messenger."
To Isaiah: He was "Salvation."
To Jeremiah: He was "Jehovah Exalts."
To Ezekiel: He was "God Strengthens."
To Daniel: He was "My Judge."
To Abraham: He was "A Friend."
To Isaac: He was "The Ram in the Bush."
To Jacob: He was "The Ladder That Reached to Heaven."
To Joseph: He was "The Coat of Many Colors."
To Moses: He was "The Burning Bush."
To David: He was "A Warrior."
To Solomon: He was "Understanding to Discern Judgment."

To Matthew: He was "The Messiah."
To Mark: He was "The Wonder Worker."
To Luke: He was "The Great Physician."
To John: He was "The Lamb of God."
To Peter: He was "The Sacrifice."
To Paul: He was "The One to Trust in for Salvation."
To James: He was "A Bond Servant."
To Thomas: He was "My Lord and My God."
To Mary Magdalene, and the Other Mary: He was "The Risen Savior."

Who is this Jesus to you, Church? I don't know who this Jesus is to you, but to me this Jesus is:

- My All-in-All
- My Bridge over Troubled Waters
- My Courtroom Lawyer
- My Doctor in a Sick Room
- My Everlasting Covenant
- My Forerunner
- My Guide
- My Healer
- My Intercessor
- My Joy Unspeakable, and Full of Glory
- My Keeper
- My Lamp
- My Mentor
- My Night Watchman
- My Offering for Sin
- My Protector from Dangers Seen and Unseen
- My Quencher of All the Fiery Darts of the Wicked One
- My Remission of Sin
- My Good Samaritan
- My Triune God
- My Undefiled Lord
- My Victorious King
- My Everlasting Witness

- My Excellent Example
- My Yoke Breaker
- My Zion, the Heavenly City

Who is this Jesus? Who is this Jesus? Church, do you know who this Jesus is? Are you sure that you know who this Jesus is? If you know who this Jesus is, why don't you help me to praise Him? Help me give Him some honor! Help me give Him some thanksgiving! Praise Him! Praise Him! Praise Him! Church, has God been good to you? Has He blessed your life? Has He made a way for you? Don't fool me now; I need a witness. If God has been good to you, raise your hands and shout, "Yes!" Shout, "Yes!" Shout, "Yes!"

Message #5

Trust in the Lord

Scripture Text: Psalm 125:1

Mount Zion is a symbol of security. The definition of the word "trust" is: firm reliance on the integrity, ability, or character of a person or thing, confident, belief, faith. On our paper money as well as on our coins there is a phrase: "In God We Trust." But I do not really think that our government really believes that, because if it were true, they would not have taken prayer out of our school system and out of various government occupations in our country today.

Today in our society, some people get offended when you say the Lord's name around them. But we, as children of God, we must not follow the world or its systems when it is in opposition to the "Word of God," because the Bible tells us that we are *in* the world, but we are not *of* the world. We don't act like the world! We don't speak like the world! We don't trust like the world!

If you don't believe me, go back with me eighty years ago, and look how the people who didn't trust in the Lord reacted to the 1929 Great Depression. I'm told people lost all of their life savings, and because they had all of their trust in their finances, when the banks closed and they could not get their money, a lot of people committed suicide. Their trust was in the wrong thing. But Church, we must continue to "Trust in the Lord."

Remember, "trust" means that we have a firm reliance on the integrity of the Lord. We have a firm reliance on the ability of the Lord. We have a firm reliance on the character of the Lord. And if we trust in the Lord like that, no matter how things may look, the Lord will provide for us, the Lord will guide and protect us, and the Lord will make a way for us. We will be like Mt. Zion, which cannot be moved.

Here are some people who put their trust in the Lord, and the results were the same; they all were victorious over their circumstances:

Daniel – when he was in the lion's den.
The Three Hebrew Boys – while in the fiery furnace.
Job – when he had lost everything.
David – when he went up against Goliath.
The Apostle Paul – when he was shipwrecked and stoned.

I could go on and on, but I have to go to my close. But I need to leave you with this advice: Church, trust in the Lord. Things may look dark and things may look bad, but keep your trust in the Lord. We may not see it now, but the Lord is working behind the scenes on our behalf, and He will make everything all right! He will! He will! Can I get a witness? If you know that He will make everything all right, shout, "Yes!" Shout, "Yes!" Shout, "Yes!"

Message #6

Let No Man Despise Your Youth

Scripture Text: 1 Timothy 4:12

I wish to thank God for the parents of these young people who bring them to the house of God! It is so very important as parents to instill the principles of worship, prayer, faith, and the importance of developing a relationship with the Lord in their young people! So parents, I salute you! And I know God will continue to bless you for bringing up your children in the fear and admonition of the Lord.

Introduction

On their first missionary journey, Paul and Barnabas preached in Lystra, a city of Lycaonia, and experienced success and persecution. It is likely that a Jewess named Lois, and her daughter, Eunice, were converted to Christ during that ministry. Eunice was married to a Gentile, by whom she had Timothy, probably an only child. Timothy evidently had been instructed in the Jewish religion, but his father refused to allow his son to be circumcised. From the beginning, a close relationship developed between Paul and Timothy.

When Paul returned to Lystra on his second journey, he found Timothy to be a member of the local church and highly recommended by its leaders there at Iconium. Under the prompting of the Holy Spirit, Paul added Timothy to his apostolic party. Since they were going to be ministering among the Jews, Paul admonished Timothy to be circumcised; not for righteousness' sake, but to avoid offending the Jews since his mother was Jewish. So this is a letter written to Timothy, a young man in the ministry by the apostle Paul.

Timothy was Paul's spiritual son, having been converted through his ministry. As young people who are born-again believers in Christ, you are to be examples of Christ in every area of your life. In other words, you are to conduct yourselves in a way that will please the Lord everywhere that you go! Paul tells young Timothy, "Let no man despise your youth." The word, "despise," means, "to regard as worthless."

Young people, there are people that you will encounter in your walk with the Lord who will despise you just because you are young. But you are always to remember that although you may be young, you are very valuable in the sight of God! God shed His precious, holy, sinless blood for you, and you are very valuable in His sight!

God has used young people all throughout the Bible! And I believe He can do, and is doing great works through our young people today. Here are a few examples of the kind of young people God can use today.

I believe God has some **Davids** who will not be afraid of the Goliaths that he will face in life, but will trust God for the victory!

I believe God has some **King Josiahs**, who was a king at the age of eight. He was a good king and he brought the people of Judah back to worshipping the true and living God!

I believe God has some **Josephs**, who was seventeen years old when he was sold into slavery by his brothers. But through all the things that he went through, he held on to God, and God brought him from the *prison* to *the palace*!

I believe God has some **Marys**, who will be obedient and humble to God's Word and will be blessed among women, knowing that with God, nothing is impossible!

I believe God has some **Esthers**, who feared the Lord, and sought God for His timing and direction, and as a result, was chosen to be queen for the sake of her people!

So young people, let no man despise your youth. Some of you have graduated from high school and are going to college. Some of you may have graduated from college and you will be joining the work force, going into your career field. Some of you will be getting promoted to the next grade level. But whatever you do in life, always put God first and I know that you will be blessed, and you will also be a blessing to others in life.

And then, when you get older and when you are talking to your children, or to the next generation of young people, if you have trusted God and put Him first in your life, you will be able to say like David in Psalm chapter 37 and verses 25-26: "I have been young, and now am old, yet have I not seen the righteous forsaken, nor his seed begging bread. He is ever merciful, and lendeth, and his seed is blessed!"

So young people, let no man despise your youth. You belong to the Lord! If you want to be successful in life, in whatever field or career you go into, put God first and live for the Lord! And God will bless your life. He will bless you more than you can ever imagine! And He will make you a blessing to others!

How many of you young people believe that today? If you do, stand up on your feet and give God some praise! Praise Him! Life Him up! Give Him glory! And always remember: Let no man...! Let no man...! Let no man despise your youth!

Message #7

What Is His Name?

Scripture Text: Proverbs 30:1-4

The words of Agur, this is a collection of proverbs written by an unknown sage, who was likely a student of wisdom at the time of Solomon. Agur reflects humility (v. 1-4), a deep hatred for arrogance (v. 7-9), and a keen theological mind (v. 5-6).

Verse 4 asks the questions: Who…and What? These questions can be answered only by revelation from God. A person can know the "what" about creative wisdom through observation of the physical world and its inner workings, but cannot know the "who." The "who" can be known only when God reveals Himself, which He has in Scripture.

Are you aware that your good name is worth a fortune? The Bible substantiates this! The wisest man who ever lived, King Solomon, wrote, "A good name is more desirable than great riches; to be esteemed is better than silver or gold" (Proverbs 22:1). Solomon also said, "A good name is better than fine perfume" (Ecclesiastes 7:1).

Why is a good name worth millions? It all traces back to God and the value He places on a name—His own and all others. In the early pages of Scripture, we gather clues about the importance of the names of God. One of the first commands given to Adam was to name the animals. When God created a helpmate for him, Adam named her Eve. But where did Adam get his name?

It makes sense that God named Adam. But God gave him a name that reflects his origin…he came from the earth. Can you imagine? Adam rises from the dirt, inhales his first gasp of air, dusts himself off, looks around, then suddenly he hears a sound—the voice of his Maker speaking his name—"Adam." That gives me chills.

When Enron, a great Texas-based energy giant and one of the leading companies in the world, is mentioned today, it brings up thoughts of greed, mismanagement, manipulation, shredding of documents, and the like.

Osama bin Laden came from a well-respected family in Saudi Arabia, known for success in construction. Now at the mention of his name, we think of terrorism, mass murder, and evil personified.

Then there are those who lived life in such a way that their names will go down in history with great integrity and respect. No matter how careful you are, sometimes circumstances and events out of your control can threaten the very integrity of a name.

God reveres His name highly. Every man, woman, boy, and girl is made in His image. It is important to Him that we treasure our own names and that we not take lightly the supreme value of a "good name."

The sword of Islam will rust.

The flower of Buddhism will wither.

The temples of Hinduism will crumble.

But the name of the Lord Jesus Christ will echo eternally as the one true God. Believers in Jesus Christ follow the Living One. He is alive today. No other faith makes this claim. When we share the name with others, we proclaim a risen Savior and a living Lord!

The name of Jesus is sweeter than honey on a honeycomb!

The name of Mohammed cannot save or deliver you.

The name of Buddha cannot save or deliver you.

Hinduism cannot save or deliver you.

Numerology cannot save or deliver you.

Scientology cannot save or deliver you.

Only Jesus can save and deliver you!

Jesus is called many names throughout the Bible. Let me tell you some of His names.

What Is His Name?

IN:	JESUS IS THE:
Genesis	Seed of the woman
Exodus	Passover Lamb
Leviticus	High Priest
Numbers	Pillar of Cloud by day and Pillar of Fire by night
Deuteronomy	Prophet like unto Moses
Joshua	Captain of Salvation
Judges	Judge and Lawgiver
Ruth	Kinsman-Redeemer
1 and 2 Samuel	Trusted Prophet
Kings and Chronicles	Reigning King
Ezra	Faithful Scribe
Nehemiah	Rebuilder of broken down wall of human life
Esther	Mordecai
Job	Ever-living Redeemer
Psalms	Shepherd
Proverbs and Ecclesiastes	Wisdom
Song of Solomon	Lover and Bridegroom
Isaiah	Prince of Peace
Jeremiah	Righteous Branch
Lamentations	Weeping Prophet
Ezekiel	Wonderful Four-Faced Man
Daniel	Fourth Man in Life's Fiery Furnaces
Hosea	Faithful Husband—Forever Married to the Backslider
Joel	Former and Latter Rain
Amos	Burden-Bearer
Obadiah	Mighty to Save
Jonah	Foreign Missionary
Micah	Messenger of Beautiful Feet
Nahum	Avenger of God's Elect
Habakkuk	God's Evangelist

Zephaniah	Fountain Opened in the House of David for Sin
Haggai	Restorer of the Lost Heritage of Israel
Zechariah	Fountain Opened in the House of Israel for Sin and Uncleanness
Malachi	Son of Righteousness with Healing in His Wings
Matthew	Messiah
Mark	Wonder-Worker
Luke	Son of Man
John	Son of God
Acts	Holy Ghost
Romans	Justifier
1 and 2 Corinthians	Sanctifier
Galatians	Redeemer from Curse of the Law
Ephesians	Christ of Unsearchable Riches
Philippians	God Who Supplies All Our Needs
Colossians	Fullness of the Godhead Bodily
1 and 2 Thessalonians	Soon Coming King
1 and 2 Timothy	Mediator Between God and Man
Titus	Faithful Pastor
Philemon	Friend Who Sticketh Closer Than a Brother
Hebrews	Blood of Everlasting Covenant
James	Great Physician
1 and 2 Peter	Chief Shepherd
1, 2, and 3 John	Love
Jude	Lord Coming with 10,000 of His Saints

Revelation . . . . King of Kings and
                                   Lord of Lords

    So Church, do you know His name?
    What is His name?
    What is His name?
    Do you love His name?
    Can I get somebody to help me praise His name? Praise Him! Praise Him! Praise Him!

Message #8

More Than a Conqueror

Scripture Text: Ephesians 6:13-17 and Romans 8:35-37

Definition of a conqueror: To defeat or subdue by force, especially by force of arms. To overcome or surmount by physical, mental, or moral force. Example: I finally conquered my fear of heights.

Famous Conquerors in History

1. **Alexander the Great (356-323 BC)** – King of Macedonia, conqueror of the Persian Empire, and one of the greatest military geniuses of all time.
2. **Genghis Khan (1167-1227)** – Mongol conqueror and founder of the Mongol empire which spanned the continent of Asia.
3. **Napoleon I (1769-1821)** – Emperor of the French, whose imperial dictatorship ended the French Revolution. One of the greatest military commanders of all time, he conquered much of Europe.
4. **General Colin Luther Powell (1937-)** – Chairman of the Joint Chiefs of Staff. He became a national figure during the successful Desert Shield and Desert Storm operations, which expelled the Iraqi army from Kuwait. His parents stressed the importance of education and personal achievement. During his military career, General Powell was awarded the Purple Heart, Bronze Star, and the Soldier's Medal. In all, he has

received eleven military decorations, including the Legion of Merit.

Young people, the question becomes, *who* or *what* shall separate you from being more than a conqueror?

Who: friends, family, peer pressure, cliques, clubs, organizations, sports teams.

What: tribulation, distress, persecution, famine, nakedness, peril, sword, being popular, social identification, bling-bling, clothes, fashion, cha-ching, or the hookups.

Young people—this is your final conflict. When you face an extreme problem, remember that you are more than conquerors in Christ when God protects you from evil. And when God delivers you and heals you, you are conquerors, because God is obviously at work. But when the problem doesn't go away, when evil does its worst, young people, remember, you are still more than conquerors.

Young people—you can be more than conquerors

- Over failure
- Over negativity
- Over your doubters
- Over your haters
- Over those who say you will not make it
- Over those who want to bring you down

"More than conquerors," what does it mean? The original word will admit a stronger rendering than some translators have allowed it. The same word is in another place rendered, "a far more and exceeding external weight of glory." So that in the present instance it might be translated, "far more exceeding conqueror." The phrase seems to imply that it is more than a mere victory which the believer gains. A battle may be won at a great loss to the conqueror. A great leader may fall at the head of his troops; the flower of any army may be destroyed; and the best blood of a nation's pride may be shed. But the Christian conquers with no such loss. Nothing whatsoever essential to his well-being is periled.

Young people, your armor is riveted upon your soul, by the Holy Spirit—you cannot lose. Your life, hidden with Christ in God, cannot be endangered. Your Leader and Commander, once dead, is alive and dies no more. Nothing valuable and precious shall you lose. There is not a grace in your soul but shall come out of the battle with sin, and Satan, and the world, purer and brighter for the conflict.

The more thoroughly the Lord brings your graces into exercise, the more fully shall they be developed, and the more mightily shall they be strengthened. Not a grain of grace shall perish in the separation of grain from the chaff. Not a particle of faith shall be consumed in the refining; losing nothing, you gain everything! You return from the battle laden with the spoils of a glorious victory, "more than a conqueror."

All your resources are increased by the result. Your armor is brighter, your sword is sharper, and your courage cannot be intimidated because of the conflict. Every grace of the spirit is matured, faith is strengthened, love is expanded, experience is deepened, and knowledge is increased. You come forth from the battle holier and more courageous than when you entered it.

"Through Him that loved us"—here is the great secret of your victory, the source of your triumph. Behold the mystery explained, how a weak, timid believer, often running from their own shadow, is yet "more than a conqueror" over their many and mighty foes.

To Christ who loved you and who gave Himself for you, who died in your stead, and lives to intercede on your behalf, the glory of the triumph is stated. And this is the song you sing, "Thanks be to God which gives us the victory through our Lord Jesus Christ." Through the conquest which He Himself obtained, through the grace which He imparts, through the strength which He inspires, through the intercession which He presents, in all of your tribulation, and distress, and persecution, and famine, and peril, and sword. Young people, you are still "more than conquerors."

Young people, when the three Hebrew children went into a burning fiery furnace, they were conquerors. But when the fourth man came and they walked out, they were "more than conquerors!"

When Daniel went into the lion's den, he was a conqueror. But when they pulled him out and made them change the laws of the Medes and Persians, he was "more than a conqueror!"

When Jesus went to the cross, He could have dispatched a legion of angels and destroyed every man that was living. He could have cursed these people, like He cursed the fig tree. But He kept His mouth shut. When He went to the grave with the sins of the world on that Friday, He was a conqueror. But when He rose from the dead on that Sunday morning, He was "more than a conqueror!"

In conclusion, the most famous conqueror of all, Jesus, the Mighty Conqueror, He conquered death, hell, and the grave! He conquered sin; He can conquer your temper, your disposition, your attitude, your habits, and your life. The devil is defeated. His dark kingdom, his domain, has no more power. Young people, you need to stand with Him, the Great, Mighty Conqueror. The Morning Star is over you! The Old Rugged Cross is before you, cleansing your ways. And if you, young people, give Jesus your life, you will be "more than a conqueror!"

Young people, do you believe it? How many of you today want to be "more than a conqueror?" Give Him praise in His house! Because of Christ, young people, you can be "more than a conqueror!"

Young People – If you know that you are "more than a conqueror," stand up and give God some praise!
Preachers – If you know that you are "more than a conqueror," stand up and give God some praise!
Deacons – If you know that you are "more than a conqueror," stand up and give God some praise!
Deaconesses – If you know that you are "more than a conqueror," stand up and give God some praise!
Musicians – If you know that you are "more than a conqueror," praise Him on the instrument!
Congregation – If you know that you are "more than a conqueror," stand up and give God some praise!
Young People – You can be "more than a conqueror!"
You can be "more than a conqueror!"
You can be "more than a conqueror!"

Message #9

Young People, God Wants You to Be an Eagle

Scripture Text: Isaiah 40:28-31

Young people, God wants you to be a success in life. He wants you to be blessed in life. He has your best interest in His heart. That's why this message is so important for you today! Today, as never before!

Young people, God wants you to be an eagle. Young people, you are living in one of the most exciting, challenging, and dangerous times in modern history. You live in a world with new pressures and problems that previous generations did not dream of. For example, here are three of them:

1 – The linking of the world economy.
2 – The growing problem of AIDS and other deadly diseases.
3 – The environmental destruction and danger.

I am not a pessimist. I believe that there is hope and there are answers, and they are all to be found in the *Word of God*!

I believe that the future belongs to eagles!

There are two kinds of people in the world: there are eagles, and there are turkeys. When America was a young nation and had won its independence from Great Britain, the leaders met to select a national bird to symbolize the character and heart of the people. America was a great nation because it had great leaders. The choice came down to two birds: the eagle or the turkey. They wisely chose the eagle.

The eagle became the symbol of our nation and symbolizes what made America great and what characterizes all great people. Eagles have always symbolized the spirit and character of the winners and champions of all nationalities—the champion, the noble of heart who rises above the storms. Eagles are the ones who will not only survive the change and winds of life, but will also thrive and prosper. The future will belong to the eagles—not the turkeys.

In America we eat turkeys, but we protect and learn from eagles. Here are four characteristics of eagles:

1. Eagles, like great leaders, are known for their character and their commitment. The eagle was chosen over the turkey because it was a noble bird, one that symbolized the character that makes leaders and eagles great!
2. Vision. Just like the eagle, all leaders must have vision. The eagle's eyes can see great distances. They can also look directly into the sun without being blinded.
3. Eagles never eat dead meat. You will never see an eagle eating meat that it did not kill. Eagles are not scavengers. They hunt and kill their own food.
4. Looks for and flies into storms. As storms approach, lesser birds head for cover. But the eagle spreads its wings and with a great cry mounts upon the powerful updrafts, soaring to heights of glory. Eagles use the storm to lift them to these great heights. Storms are challenges to the Christian. We don't run from them! To eagles, storms are tools used for their development.

So young people, you must understand that spiritual strength comes from waiting upon the Lord! And if you wait on the Lord, He will make you an eagle!

In conclusion, young people, there is an old saying that goes: "Birds of a feather flock together." If you are going to be an eagle, you cannot hang out with turkeys, simply because *eagles don't hang out with turkeys...period!* And by turkeys, I'm talking about people who do not want to make a positive impact in society; people who want to hold you back because they don't want to improve their lives, and they don't want you to improve your life. They have no positive goals for their lives. They are negative thinkers, and they do not want anything to do with *God*!

Young people, I am here to tell you that you cannot afford to be influenced by them because you are an eagle! With *God* all things are possible! You are an *eagle*! *God* created you to be successful in life; to bring about a positive impact in society, as well as to bring Him praise and glory! So remember, young people,

God wants you to be an eagle!
God wants you to be an eagle!
God wants you to be an eagle!

Message #10

Young People, Everything Is Going to Be All Right

Scripture Text: 2 Kings 4:16-26

This story is about the prophet Elisha and the Shunammite woman. Elisha was blessed by her and her husband. They made him a little chamber, or a room, because he would pass by their house quite a lot, so they made him a room where he could rest and refresh himself when he came their way. (It is good to do good things for the man of God.)

The man of God said to her, "You have been so good to me. What can I do for you?" And Gehazi, Elisha's servant, told Elisha that she was without a child. So Elisha called for the woman and prophesized over her saying, "About this season, according to the time of life, thou shalt have a son." And as prophesized, the woman had a child (son).

And when the child was grown, it fell on a day that he went out to his father and to the reapers. Then he said to his father, "My head, my head." And the father told another young man to carry him to his mother. And when he had taken him and brought him to his mother, he sat on her knees till noon, and then died. And the mother took her dead son and laid him on the bed of the man of God, and shut the door upon him and went out.

She then called to her husband and said to him, "Send me, I pray thee, one of the young men and one of the colts, that I may run to the man of God and come again." So she went up to the man of

God, to Mount Carmel, and when the man of God saw her afar off, he said to Gehazi, his servant, "Behold, yonder is that Shunammite. Run now, I pray thee, to meet her and say unto her, 'Is it well with thee? Is it well with thy husband? Is it well with thy child?'" And she answered, *"It is well!"* In other words, she knew that everything was going to be all right. And from verse 26, I will use as my subject: "Young people, everything is going to be all right."

"Young people, everything is going to be all right."

Remember now thy Creator in the days of thy youth, while the evil days come not, nor the years draw nigh, when thou shalt say, I have no pleasure in them (Ecclesiastes 12:1).

And they brought young children to Him, that He should touch them: and His disciples rebuked those that brought them. But when Jesus saw it, He was much displeased, and said unto them, "Suffer the little children to come unto Me, and forbid them not: for of such is the Kingdom of God" (St. Mark 10:13-14).

And he said, "All these have I kept from my youth up" (St. Luke 18:21).

Let no man despise thy youth; but be thou an example of the believers, in word, in conversation, in charity, in spirit, in faith, in purity (1 Timothy 4:12).

These Scriptures were not just inspired by God for nothing. But they tell me how much God really loves and how much He is concerned about young people.

Young people, in our world today, a lot of things are taking place. The AIDS virus is plaguing the nation at a high rate. Crime is running rampant amount our youth. Teen pregnancies and abortions are at an all-time high. The number of kids dropping out of high school is increasing. Young people are dying at a growing rate of speed. Our young people are spending more time in front of the television set and watching violent and unwholesome programs, and they are listening to music that is saturated with lyrics that come from the very pit of hell itself. Our young people are raising themselves, due to the economy, in which the majority of households, both parents have to work.

Young people, everything is going to be all right!

I know that young people today, you have a hard time. I know some of you might have been hurt; some of you are hurting right now. I know that it seems that you are on the short end of the stick. I know that you are faced with a lot of challenges and temptations. I know that you are sometimes misunderstood. I know that some of you may feel that you should not have been born. I know that you sometimes feel left out and alone.

But I'm not here to criticize you or to put you down. I'm here to encourage you, to lift you up, and pull you up out of the mind-set that the enemy has put you in. I'm here with a message of hope, to tell you what the Word of God says. And the Word of God tells me that everything is going to be all right!

I'm also here to tell you that regardless of what the world is doing, you do not have to bow down to peer pressure. Young people, you do not have to follow or do what everybody else is doing!

I'm told in the Bible there were three young men: one named Shadrach; one named Meshach; and one named Abednego. They were told by King Nebuchadnezzar that when they heard the sounds of all kinds of music, they were supposed to fall down and worship this image of gold that was made. These three young men were raised differently. They were raised to worship only the one true, living God of Israel! These three young men were told that if they did not bow, they would burn in a fiery furnace. But these three young men had made up their minds; they would not bow down!

Young people, in this Christian life, you have to have a made-up mind, and you also have to take a stand for the Lord! These three young men refused to bow down before the image, and the king was going to have them thrown into the fiery furnace. But before they went in, I believe they said, "King, no matter what you do to us, you can throw us into the fiery furnace, but we just want you to know that everything is going to be all right! Because the God that we serve is able to deliver us out of your hand! And even if He does not, everything is going to be all right! Because our God can deliver!

Young people, know this, that you don't have to bow down to the enemy; you don't have to raise up the white flag of surrender! Because there is a God who can deliver!

In the Gospel of St. Matthew, chapter 7 and verses 24-27, it tells about the parable of the two builders. One built his house on the sand (which are the worldly things and the world's system), and the other builder built his house on the rock, or in other words, on the solid foundation. Jesus Christ, the sure foundation; Jesus Christ, the solid rock!

Young people, be sure to understand, that no matter which foundation you build on, the rains of life will fall upon your house; the winds of discouragement, despair, and delusions will blow upon your house; the waves of fear, trouble, and tribulation will beat upon your house. And if you have built your house on the right foundation, your house shall be able to stand! That's why the songwriter said *on Christ!* Not on drugs, not on money, not on cars, not on houses, or not on land, but *on Christ, the solid Rock, I stand; all other ground is sinking sand!*

I'm encouraging you, young people, today, to build on Jesus! He will not fail you! He will not let you down! Trust in Him, and depend on Him! And everything is going to be all right!

Young people, you must establish your relationship with God while you are young, before the evils of life harden your heart. Young people, if you want to be blessed, you must obey the Lord. The Bible says, "to obey is better than sacrifice" (1 Samuel 15:22).

Young people, don't allow movie stars, rock stars, or sports stars, to be your role models, but rather let Jesus Christ be your role model, for He is the perfect role model. Don't let sex, drugs, alcohol, teenage pregnancies, or other types of perversions control and guide you, but follow the truth. Jesus said, "I am the way, the truth, and the life" (St. John 14:6)!

I'm here to tell you, young people, that Buddha is not the way.

I'm here to tell you, young people, that Mohammed is not the way.

I'm here to tell you, young people, that Hare Krishna is not the way.

The Virgin Mary is not the way.

Dr. Moon is not the way. You have to go higher than the moon! You have to get to the "Son!" I'm talking about Jesus Christ, the Son of the living God!

Young people, you must take the right direction. Make sure you are on the right road. You can take U. S. 19 north and get to Tallahassee. You can take I-95 north and get to New York. You can head down I-75 south and go across Alligator Alley to get to Miami. You can take I-4 east to get to Orlando. But if you want to go to heaven, you cannot take U. S. 19 north, I-75 south, I-4 east, or I-95 north. But you have to take Route 66! I'm talking about from Genesis to Revelation. You have to obey the Word of God. The Word of God is your road map from earth to heaven!

The psalmist David said in Psalm 37:25: "I have been young, and now I am old; yet have I never seen the righteous forsaken, nor his seed begging bread." I'm here to tell you, young people, that if you put your trust in God, God will never leave you or forsake you! God will make a way for you, and He will always be there for you.

Young people, I also want you to know that in today's world, especially in the medical field, we have doctors who specialize in certain areas of medicine. You have ear specialists, your eye specialists, your nose specialists, blood specialists, heart specialists, and many other specialists. But I want to tell you that God specializes in all areas of life—physical, financial, and spiritual! God specializes in body aches and pains. God specializes in habits, in faith, in hunger, in discomfort, in trouble, in salvation. A songwriter sang a song and the song is entitled, "God Specializes." It says God specializes and He will do what no other power, Holy Ghost power, no other power can do!

Young people, you must understand that spiritual strength does not come by physically working out with weights, or physically jogging, or any other physical exercises. But spiritual strength comes from *waiting* upon the Lord. Can somebody say, "Amen!"? That's why the Bible says, "Even the youths shall faint and be weary, and the young men shall utterly fall: But they that wait upon the Lord shall renew their strength; they shall mount up with wings as eagles; they shall run, and not be weary; and they shall walk, and not faint" (Isaiah 40:30-31).

There is a song that says: You can't hurry God. No, no, no, you just have to wait. You got to trust Him and give Him time, no matter how long it takes. He's a God that you can't hurry. He'll be there, don't you worry. He may not come when you want Him, but He'll be on time! The Bible also says in the book of Romans, chapter 8 and verse 28: "And we know that all things work together for good to them that love God, to them who are called according to His purpose."

Young people, things may not always go just right. Sometimes the going may seem tough, but remember what the Bible says in Psalm 34:19, "Many are the afflictions of the righteous: but the Lord delivereth him out of them all."

Young people, if you trust in the Lord, you can be assured of some hard times, suffering, persecutions, and afflictions, but God said He will deliver you out of them all. In other words, everything is going to be all right!

In Romans 8:35-37, young people, a question is asked, "Who shall separate us from the love of Christ? Shall tribulation, or distress, or persecution, or famine, or nakedness, or peril, or sword? As it is written, For thy sake we are killed all the day long; we are accounted as sheep for the slaughter. Nay in all these things we are more than conquerors through him that loved us."

Young people, no matter what you are going through, if you love the Lord, and if you are walking with Him, you will be more than conquerors through Christ Jesus who loves you!

There is a story in the Bible when Jesus was on a ship with His disciples. Jesus was asleep in the ship when all of a sudden they were in a storm. The disciples were afraid to the point that they woke up Jesus, who asked them, "Where is your faith?" Then Jesus told the wind and the waves, "Peace, be still!" And immediately there was a great calm!

Young people, I want you to know that when Jesus is on board...! When Jesus is on the ship, no matter how the winds may blow...! No matter how hard the waves may beat against the ship...! Remember, as long as Jesus is on board, everything will be all right!

The Bible tells me of the story of Paul and Silas. They were in prison locked up (Acts 16:25-26). The Bible says that at midnight

Paul and Silas prayed, and sang praises unto God, and the prisoners heard them. And suddenly there was a great earthquake, so that the foundations of the prison were shaken. And immediately all the doors were opened, and everyone's bands were loosed.

Young people, after you have prayed, after you have given the Lord your petition, begin to give God praise. The Bible says that the prisoners heard Paul and Silas pray and praise God! Don't be afraid of what other people may say or think. There's power in praise! Praising God will set you free! Some of you young people are in prison. I'm not talking about a physical prison, but a spiritual prison. You are imprisoned by fear, by hopelessness, by drugs, by sins that you have committed. But I'm here to tell you, if you start praising God, God will set you free! He will send a spiritual earthquake in your life, and you will be set free! God will shake open your prison doors!

Praising God will cause every chain of bondage to drop off of you! How many of you here tonight want to be set free? If you do, stand up on your feet and praise God! I don't know about you, but by reading His Word, it tells me that He is worthy to be praised!

The apostle John gives us a scene in heaven in Revelation chapter 4, and verse 8. He says: "And the four beasts had each of them six wings about him; and they were full of eyes within: and they rest not day and night, saying, Holy, holy, holy, Lord God Almighty, which was, and is, and is to come."

And then in the tenth and eleventh verses of Revelation, chapter 4, it says: The four and twenty elders fall down before him that sat on the throne, and worship him that liveth for ever and ever, and cast their crowns before the throne, saying, Thou art worthy, O Lord, to receive glory and honour and power: for thou hast created all things, and for thy pleasure they are and were created.

Young people, God says everything is going to be all right! That's why He died, because the Bible says that Jesus endured the cross, despising the shame. Why? Because of the joy that was set before Him! In other words, Jesus knew that everything was going to be all right! How many of you here tonight believe that if we trust God and live for Him, that everything is going to be all right? If you believe it, stand up on your feet and praise the living God!

Praise Him! Worship Him! Adore Him! Shout, "Hallelujah!" Shout, "Thank You, Jesus!" Tell the Lord that you love Him! Tell the Lord that you love Him!

I'm glad that I serve a God who sits high and looks low! I'm glad that my God is the King of Kings and the Lord of Lords! I'm glad that because my God is running the show, I know! I know! Church, I said, "I know!" That everything is going to be all right! If you believe that everything is going to be all right, shout, "Yes!" Shout, "Yes!" Shout, "Yes!

Message #11

Hope Beyond This Life

Scripture Text: 1 Corinthians 15:19

1 Corinthians 15:19
If in this life only we have hope in Christ, we are of all men most miserable.

May the Lord bless those who will hear and obey His written and divine words.

The title of this message is: "Hope Beyond This Life." Hope beyond this life. On Christ, the solid Rock, I stand; all other ground is sinking sand. Church, did you hear me? I said, "On Christ, the solid Rock, I stand; all other ground is sinking sand." This statement tells me that my only hope is in Jesus! Can somebody say, "Amen!"?

The Greek word for hope is *elpis*. This original word means, "A joyful and contented expectation of eternal salvation." A second meaning of the word "hope" is: to look forward to with confidence of fulfillment. In this chapter of 1 Corinthians, the apostle Paul hypothetically assumes the false premise of no resurrection to show its far-reaching implication.

Christianity completely depends on the real, physical resurrection of the dead body of Christ; otherwise it is all a lie. The purpose of this epistle of 1 Corinthians is a pastoral letter, written to resolve doctrinal and practical problems within the local church. Paul's authorship gives the letter apostolic application to all "the churches of God."

The apostle Paul states that, "Due to the resurrection of Christ from the dead, we, the believers, have a hope." The Word of God applies to us today, as well as the church of Corinth. Take a look at the people around you in the world. They look lifeless, they look joyless, and they look hopeless. But as children of the Most High God, we should be full of life, we should be full of joy, and we should be full of hope, because our hope is not in the world or in the world's system! But our hope is built on nothing less, but Jesus Christ's blood and His righteousness.

The sons of Korah declared in Psalm 43 and verse 5, "Why art thou cast down, O my soul? And why art thou disquieted?" or in other words, "Why are you being deprived of peace and rest within me?" "Hope in God; for I shall yet praise Him, who is the health of my countenance, and my God."

I read last weekend in the paper about a teenage girl in California who murdered her nine-pound newborn baby boy; and after killing her baby, she then threw the baby's body into a neighbor's yard, which had two pit bulls in the yard—an adult pit bull and a puppy pit bull. The puppy pit bull attacked and mauled the body of the newborn baby boy! What a shame; what a pity.

And also recently we heard of a lady in South Carolina who let her two boys drown to death by having them both secured in car seats in the back seat of the car, and letting the car down a boat ramp in a lake. A mother who took the lives of her two sons—what a pity, and what a shame. The mother in each of these stories obviously did not know about the God of hope!

We are living in a world of hopelessness!

We are living in a world where people are unkind!

We are living in a world where some people are cold and unfriendly!

We are living in a world of uncontrollable crime!

We are living in a world of confusion!

We are living in a world where God is not worshipped and praised as He ought to be!

We are living in a world where people purposely break the laws of the land!

We are living in a world where people will love you today, and hate you tomorrow!

We are living in a world where right is called wrong, and wrong is called right!

We are living in a world where our own children are not even safe in school due to the fact that some other kid may bring a gun to school and start shooting up the classroom.

We are living in a world where our own children are not safe at the school's bus stops due to the fact that they might get kidnapped.

We are living in a world where you have to be a prisoner in your own home. You have to put all kinds of locks on your doors.

We are living in a world where you have to pay bills or else they will turn off your water and they will turn off your lights!

We are living in a world where if you miss a house payment they will come and put you out of your own house, and they will set your furniture out on the streets.

We are living in a world where some people do not believe that Jesus was crucified, was buried, and was resurrected on the third day by God the Father. That's why the apostle Paul said in our Scripture lesson: "If in this life only we have hope in Christ, we are all men most miserable." But I'm glad, that as children of the Most High God, our hope is in the God who spoke this world into existence!

Our hope is in the God who said, "Let there be light," and there has been light ever since!

Our hope is in the God who will make a way when there seems to be *no way.*

Our hope is in the God who knows the number of the stars in the universe!

Our hope is in the God who delivered the children of Israel from the hands of Pharaoh!

Our hope is in the God who delivered the three Hebrew boys from the fiery furnace!

Our hope is in the God who delivered Daniel from the lion's den!

Our hope is in the God who holds the future in His hands!

Our hope is in the God who holds our breath in His hands!
Our hope is in the God who holds the whole world in His hands!
Our hope is in the God who can speak to the winds and the waves and they obey Him!
Our hope is in the God who can speak to the storms in our lives and there will be peace!
Our hope is in the God who is the solid Rock!
Our hope is in the God who is the true vine!
Our hope is in the God who is faithful!
Our hope is in the God who is our shepherd!
Our hope is in the God who is our healer!
Our hope is in the God who is our provider!
Our hope is in the God who is our righteousness!
Our hope is in the God who promises to never leave us or forsake us!
Our hope is in the God who is the second Adam!
Our hope is in the God who is the Ancient of days!
Our hope is in the God who is the amen, the faithful, and true witness!
Our hope is in the God who is the apostle of our profession!
Our hope is in the God who is the bread of life!
Our hope is in the God who is the bright and morning star!
Our hope is in the God who is the chief cornerstone!
Our hope is in the God who is the commander!
Our hope is in the God who is the daystar!
Our hope is in the God who is the consolation of Israel!
Our hope is in the God who is the diadem!
Our hope is in the God who is the costly cornerstone!
Our hope is in the God who is the good master!
Our hope is in the God who is the mighty one of Jacob!
Our hope is in the God who is the shoot of the stem of Jesse!
Our hope is in the God who is the seed of David!
Our hope is in the God who is the ruler in Israel!
Our hope is in the God who is the purifier and refiner!
Our hope is in the God who is the most mighty!
Our hope is in the God who is the minister of the sanctuary!
Our hope is in the God who is the King of Zion!

Our hope is in the God who is the light of the Gentiles!
Our hope is in the God who is the Lord of all!
Our hope is in the God who is the unspeakable gift!
Oh, I'm so glad today, Church, that my hope is built on Jesus!
Church, I said, "I'm glad that my hope is built on Jesus!"
Church, is your hope built on Jesus?
Church, is your hope built on Jesus?
If it is, raise your hands and shout, "Yes! Yes! Yes!"
We have a hope!
We have a lively hope!
Not because the Democrats or the Republicans are in office!
Not because a certain person is the president!
But because *Jesus is Lord!*
Jesus is Lord!
Jesus is Lord!
Jesus is Lord!
"Hope beyond this life!"

Message #12

The Blood of Jesus

Scripture Text: Colossians 1:14

Our Scripture lesson is found in the book of Colossians, chapter 1, verse 14, which reads:

In whom we have redemption through his blood, even the forgiveness of sins.

May the Lord bless those who will hear and obey His words. The title of this message is, "The Blood of Jesus."

The blood of Jesus. When we think of blood, what do we think about? First of all, what is blood? Let's define blood. Blood is the fluid which circulates in the arteries and veins of an animal—the circulatory life fluid of the body. The life is in the blood. The blood is actually the basis of the physical life.

Is blood precious to us? Why is blood precious to us? It must be precious to us because we don't like to lose it. Some of us don't like to give it. By a show of hands, how many in here don't mind giving blood to someone else? Now I know some of you might be afraid of being stuck by needles. But if a close relative or best friend's life depended upon your blood to live, how many of you would be willing to give the blood, regardless of the pain of a needle?

Does blood speak? I say, yes, it does! Blood speaks. In Genesis chapter 4, verses 9 and 10, it says:

And the Lord said unto Cain, Where is Abel thy brother? And he said, I know not: am I my brother's keeper? And he said, what hast thou done? The voice of thy brother's blood crieth unto me from the ground.

When a person is gunned down, stabbed to death, or murdered without a cause, do you think that person's blood cries out to God for justice? I believe that it does. Think of all the babies that have been murdered through abortion. I believe that those God-given lives that God intended to be brought forth into this world didn't get that chance. I know their blood cries out to the Heavenly Father, and God will revenge them, because He is a God of justice; He is a God of purpose; and He is a God of holiness!

Blood guarantees unity; the blood guarantees our unity. Every twenty-three seconds your blood makes a complete loop from the heart, carrying nutrients and oxygen, cleansing the whole body. It keeps moving and circulating. The moment it stops moving, you die. Blood is what keeps your body together. So it is in the Body of Christ. We are members of one body. Denominations divide; the blood of Jesus unifies.

To those of us who preach the glorious Gospel of Jesus Christ and the blood of Jesus, it is the blood of Jesus that gives power to our Gospel. The blood of Jesus gives life and anointing to our teaching. Without the blood of Jesus, there is no salvation. Without the blood of Jesus, there is no deliverance from Satan's power. Without the blood of Jesus, there is no hope of everlasting life.

We are not saved by church membership. We are not saved by baptism in water. Church membership and baptism in water are no more than empty religious experiences if you have not had the blood of Jesus applied to your heart.

We are not saved by membership in fraternal orders and/or by doing good works. We are not saved by our morality or our respectability. God cares nothing at all about your goodness. All of your righteousness is as "filthy rags" if the blood of Jesus has not been applied to your heart. Do you think a loving God put His Son through the agony and pain of the cross just so He could write something in

Matthew, Mark, Luke, and John that would touch you emotionally? *Never!*

The only thing in your physiological structure that moves is the blood. When the blood stops moving, you die immediately. There is an analogy with the blood of Christ and the Body of Christ, the Church. When the blood of Christ, which is our unity, stops moving, the church dies. The church that does not have the blood of Jesus Christ as its prime mover is a dead church; it is a religious country club.

The man who prays without the blood of Jesus Christ covering that prayer is going through a religious ritual without life or power. Without the blood of Jesus Christ, your testimony is nothing but empty words; it won't clear the roof and certainly will not threaten Satan or his powers and principalities. It is the blood of Jesus Christ that gives life to our prayer, life to our church, life to our teaching, life to our preaching, and life to the Gospel.

In a few moments we're going to take communion. What is communion? It is, symbolically, a blood transfusion from the throne of grace. When Jesus gave the cup to His disciples at the Lord's Supper, He said, "This is my blood of the new testament, which is shed for many for the remission of sins. Drink ye all of it (Matthew 26:27-28).

Why do we need this divine blood transfusion? Because Adam died with blood poisoning, and that poisoning, the virus of sin, is in the blood. When Adam sinned, his spiritual relationship with God died. There has been a sin virus in the blood from that time until now. But today when we lift that communion cup, we are symbolically taking in the supernatural, life-changing blood of Jesus Christ.

Any medical doctor will tell you that right now in your body there are viruses running loose. Some of you have cancer cells moving through your body right now. You don't know it, but they are there. By the time medical science can detect cancer, it's too late. It's been there too long. Because of the power of the blood, I believe that when you lift that communion cup to your lips, cancerous cells begin to die by the healing power of the resurrected Son of God. The AIDS virus will come under divine authority in the presence of the communion cup. The life is in the blood and it comes from the throne of God.

"Drink ye all of it." The apostle Paul said when you drink the cup unworthily, you drink unto yourself damnation (1 Corinthians 11:29). And for this reason, he said, "many are sick and weakly among you and many sleep (1 Corinthians 11:30). When you lift the communion cup to your lips and your life is not right with God, you are mocking the cross and the blood of Jesus Christ, and God's wrath is poured out upon you.

When you lift the communion cup to your lips, it is not just a ceremony; it is the foundation of a relationship. What you are saying is, "There is nothing between my soul and my Savior." If the blood of Jesus Christ is not over the doorpost of your heart, Satan can still rob, kill, and destroy. He can get through your morality. He can get through your goodness. He can get through all of your love of mankind through your benevolence. The one thing he cannot penetrate is the blood of Jesus Christ. If you will apply the blood of Jesus to your life today, you can live!

Jesus Christ was the perfect sacrificial lamb, and when He died on Calvary's cross, my sins and your sins died with Him. The blood of the sacrificial Lamb flows through the pages of the New Testament. It tumbles through the book of Acts. It spills through the book of Romans. It flows through the pages of Corinthians, Galatians, Ephesians, Philippians, Colossians, Thessalonians, Timothy, Titus, Philemon, Hebrews, James, 1 and 2 Peter, 1, 2, and 3 John, Jude, and then John the revelator concludes: "Unto him that loved us, and washed us from our sins in his own blood, and hath made us kings and priests unto God and his Father; to him be glory and dominion for ever and ever. Amen" (Revelation 1:5-6).

The blood of Jesus cried mercy for us on Calvary's cross. We were all as guilty as foxes in a chicken coop, with feathers all around our mouth. Sin separated us from the light of the glorious Gospel of the Prince of Glory! But Jesus, our high priest, shed His sinless blood on the judgment seat for us, and the blood cries mercy.

What blinds most people to this simple truth is a lack of understanding about the very thing they seek. Sin-infected humanity needed the kind of blood transfusion only God could provide. And

The Blood of Jesus

the only way such a divine exchange could be made was if God Himself provided the blood.

In 1 Peter, chapter 1, verses 18 and 19, the apostle Peter is speaking to the dispersed Jewish believers in various parts of Asia Minor, who were suffering rejection in the world because of their obedience to Christ. He exorts them, and this same exhortation applies to us today, and it says:

> Forasmuch as ye know that ye were not redeemed with corruptible things, as silver and gold, from your vain conversation received by tradition from your fathers. But with the precious blood of Christ, as of a lamb without blemish and without spot.

It didn't take shining silver or yellow gold to purchase our redemption. But it took the precious blood of our Lord Jesus Christ! The spotless, sinless Lamb of God! And because of His shed blood on Calvary's cross, we have life! We have a hope! We have victory! We have blessings! We have joy! We have peace! We can shout, "Glory!" We can shout, "Hallelujah!" We can shout, "Thank You, Jesus!" We can sing, "How Great Thou Art"! How many of you here are glad for the blood of Jesus? How many of you here are glad that Jesus shed His blood for you?

I don't know about you, but I know that I am glad about the blood of Jesus! I'm so glad that He shed His holy blood for me! Church, are you glad about it? How many of you are really glad about it? If you are glad about it, raise your hands and shout, "Yes! Yes! Yes!"

We all were once in sin. We were at one time in our life in bondage. We were once in the prison of sin. Satan had the key to the prison and he would not let us out. The blood of goats could not pay the price for our freedom. The blood of bulls didn't have the power to free us from our bondage of sin. The blood of pigeons could not pay our bond of sin. The blood of turtledoves could not get us out of our prison cell. The blood of all the patriarchs could not do the job. But there was One who came in the volume of the book! His name is called Jesus! Jesus! His blood was able to set us free! His blood has the power to pay our bond of sin! His blood has the power to wash us whiter than snow! If you are glad about it, shout, "Yes! Yes! Yes! Yes!"

Message #13

Heaven or Hell: The Choice Is Yours

Scripture Text: St. Luke 16:19-21
Reference Scriptures: St. Luke 6:41-42; St. Luke 12:16-21; Hebrews 9:27; Isaiah 64:6; St. John 5:28-29; Revelation 20:12-15

This is a sermon that is not one to make you happy. It is not a sermon designed to entertain you. It is not a sermon designed to make you shout and scream. But it is a sermon designed for you to think. It is designed to make each one of us conduct a spiritual inventory upon ourselves. It is time that we hear the Word of the Lord! So I want us to put on our spiritual ears and put on our spiritual eyes so that we can be ready to absorb the Word of God. I want each of us to let the Word of God fall on good ground, so that it will take root and grow.

In life we all are given choices, choices to make in all areas of our lives. We have to choose to obey our parents, or not to obey our parents; to obey the law, or not to obey the law; to be successful in life, or not to be successful in life; to obey God, or not to obey God. And with each choice that we make in our lives, there are consequences that follow.

Where will you spend eternity? In heaven? Or in hell? These are the only choices available. We all are going to spend eternity in one of these places.

How many here today would like to go to heaven? Raise your hands, please.

How many here today would like to go to hell? Raise your hands, please.

Well, there are some things that you must do in order to go to heaven.

If you want to go to heaven, you must be born again (St. John 3:3)! You must live holy. You must be led by the Spirit of God, because the Bible says, "To as many as are led by the Spirit of God, they are the sons of God (Romans 8:14). We must live the Word of God, because the Bible says that the devils or demons also believe and tremble (James 2:19). And if you want to go to hell, just do the exact opposite. Heaven or hell! The choice is yours.

Now the definition of the word *choice* is: to select, option, the power or right to choose or select. In the book of Joshua, chapter 24 and verse 15, it says, "Choose this day whom you will serve." Joshua asked the children of Israel that question. Church, do you love the Lord? Church, do you believe the Bible? Do you really? If you really believe the Bible, then you will believe that heaven is as real as you are sitting in your seat in this church today. And if you really believe the Bible, then you will believe that hell is as real as you are sitting in your seat, breathing your very breath!

Jesus spoke more about hell than He did about heaven. You may be very religious and still go to hell. If you don't believe me, remember the Pharisees. You can be morally good and still go to hell. You can go to church every day of your life and still be eternally lost. We do not know when we will leave this earth. So we need to know where we will spend eternity. We need to know the way.

You may know how to get to New York. You may know important people. You may know wealth, riches, and power. But if you do not know Jesus as your personal Lord and Savior, you are lost; you are condemned. You are hell bound!

Jesus, who is the only way of salvation, wants you and me to give Him our lives so that we don't have to be lost for all eternity. The Bible calls hell, where there is weeping, wailing, and gnashing of teeth, where the worm dieth not and the fire is never quenched (St. Mark 9:44,46,48).

Some of us say that we are Christians and love God, yet we hate each other. Something is wrong, for the Bible tells me in the book of 1 John, chapter 4 and verse 20, "If a man say, I love God, and hateth his brother, he is a liar: for he that loveth not his brother whom he hath seen, how can he love God whom he hath not seen?"

We need to come clean. We need to repent of our sins and get right with God. If you have ought against your brother, the Bible says that before we offer our gift to God on the altar, lay your gift down and go get things straightened out between you and your brother. And after you have done this, then you can come and offer your gift to the Lord (St. Matthew 5:23-24); because if we do not get things right with our sisters and brothers, our prayers will not be answered.

And until we forgive one another, God will not forgive us, no matter how much we come to church and put on a front, as if we are so holy. No matter how much money you give or how long you may pray, no matter what you may do, until you and I forgive each other, God cannot and will not forgive us, and we will not be blessed with the blessings of the Lord.

Did you know that you are in debt because of your sin (Romans 3:23)?

Do you realize what the cost of your sin debt will bring in eternity (Romans 6:23a; Revelation 20:14)?

Have you heard? Your sin debt has been "paid in full" (St. Matthew 1:21; 1 Peter 3:18a; St. John 19:30).

Will you believe the Bible, the record of what God has done for you (1 Timothy 1:15a; 1 John 5:11-12)?

Will you trust the eternity of your soul completely to Jesus Christ (St. John 3:16; Acts 13:39; Acts 16:31b)?

I choose to trust Jesus Christ and His finished payment for my sin debt (Acts 10:43; Romans 10:9-10; Romans 10:13).

I choose to reject the payment of Jesus Christ and trust my payment (Hebrews 2:3a; 2 Thessalonians 1:7-9).

Remember, the choice is yours.

Good or evil.

Blessings or cursings.

Life or death.

Heaven or hell.

Christ or Satan.

The narrow way or the broad way.

Jesus said that there are two roads in life. He said that one is a broad road that leads to judgment and destruction and hell. On that road people seem to be having a wonderful time, and it is the road that is travelled the most.

Then Jesus said that there is a narrow road, and we enter it by a narrow gate. He said that it leads to heaven. Traveling on that road is difficult because we go against the tide of history, the tide of all the pleasures and the sins of this world, and it is the road that is traveled the least (St. Matthew 7:13-14).

Dear friend, please listen to me.

You may not believe the sky is blue, but it is!

You may not believe that fire burns, but it does!

You may not believe that you will have to die one day, but you will!

You may not believe that after death comes the judgment, but it does!

You may not believe that one day you will stand before a holy, righteous God and give an account for your life, but you will!

So I plead with you to accept Jesus Christ into your heart and make Him Savior and Lord of your life, before it is too late!

Remember, it is not Jesus and Mohammed that will save you!

It is not Jesus and Buddha that will save you!

It is not Jesus and good works that will save you!

It is only Jesus that can save you! Only Jesus!

Buddha and Mohammed are still buried in their graves, but it is only Jesus' tomb that is empty, and that is because He lives! He lives! He rose from the grave on the third day and He lives forevermore! Remember, eternity is too long of a time to be separated from the Lord Jesus Christ!

Message #14

It's Time for the Redeemed of the Lord Say So

Introduction

The book of Psalms is a compilation of several ancient collections of Hebrew songs and poetry for use in congregational worship, as well as in private devotion. In some collections the ancient compilers gathered together, mostly David's superb songs. In others they drew from a variety of authors such as Moses, Asaph, Heman, the sons of Korah, Solomon, Ethan, and Jeduthun. Many of the psalms are from unnamed sources. Jewish scholars called these "orphan psalms." The book of Psalms, division 107, is a psalm of deliverance.

The psalms can be divided into five books, exactly like the first five books of the Old Testament: Genesis, Exodus, Leviticus, Numbers, and Deuteronomy. These five books are called the "Pentateuch." The first five books of the Old Testament correspond to the five divided books of Psalms.

Book #1 – Psalms 1:1-41:13 are called the "Genesis" psalms where man was seen in a state of blessedness, fall, and recovery.

Book #2 – Psalms 42:1-72:20 are the "Exodus" psalms where man was seen in ruin and redemption (Israel in view).

Book #3 – Psalms 73:1-89:52 are the "Leviticus" psalms where the sanctuary was in view, darkness and dawn.

Book #4 – Psalms 90:1-106:48 are the "Numbers" psalms where the earth is in view, peril and protection.

Book #5 – Psalms 107:1-150:6 are the "Deuteronomy" psalms where there is perfection and praise of the Word of God.

This is the Y. W. A.'s challenge service, and in order for all of us to understand what this is all about, let's define a few words so that all of us will be on the same level.

Challenge – This word means to summon to action, effort or use, to stimulate.
Let – This word means to grant permission, to allow.
Redeemed – This word means to buy back.
Say – This word means to speak, to express in words, to state, or to declare.

God said in the beginning of creation, when there was nothing but darkness and chaos, "let" there be light and there was light! In another occasion in the book of Exodus, God told Moses to tell Pharaoh to "let" my people go. We must preach the uncompromising Gospel of Jesus Christ to more people so that those in the world can hear the message of salvation. There's never been a time in our nation's history when we needed the Gospel preached more than today.

But first of all, in order for the redeemed to "say so," you must have something to say! So here are three questions that I am going to ask for all of us who are redeemed to ponder on, and for all of the redeemed to take a spiritual inventory of ourselves.

Question #1 – What are we saying to the world?
Question #2 – What are we saying to one another?
Question #3 – What kind of effect is it having on the household of faith and the world?

If you want to be popular, or if you want to be the favorite, or if you want to be a people pleaser, then do not accept the challenge. Sometimes you will have to do like David. The Bible says that David encouraged himself in the Lord (1 Samuel 30:6).

You will have to make up your mind that: I am going on with the Lord; I am going on with the Lord. I am determined to make heaven my eternal home, even if I have to go all by myself.

Whether or not my grandmother goes, or my grandfather goes, or my mother goes, or my father goes. Whether or not my sisters go, or my brothers go. Whether or not my uncles go, or my aunts go. Whether or not my cousins go, or my nieces go, or my nephews go. Whether or not my children go, or my godchildren go, my good friends go. Whether or not my husband goes, or the wife goes, or the girlfriend goes, or the boyfriend goes. We must be determined to go with the Lord all the way. Why? Because we are the redeemed of God! And we are going all the way, in Jesus' name!

We need more "say so" Christians. Let the redeemed of the Lord say so. Don't go around complaining and criticizing. If you are a Christian, tell others how good God is. He is good, but He doesn't have a good name in the world today. God's reputation is bad.

A reputation is what people think of you. God does not have many friends in court among the multitudes of people in the world; no champion or defender, and few to testify on His behalf. There are a few to take the witness stand and say a good word in His behalf. If you doubt that, look around.

Consider the pagan and heathen religions. Their conception of God is terrifying. He is pictured as a god that will destroy, not save; a god that is difficult to approach, and takes no personal interest in his creatures, nor does he love them. The average person today lives in a world in a land with a veneer of civilization; in other words, an outward show that enhances, but misrepresents what lies beneath. The average person today lives with a modicum of education; in other words, a small or moderate amount of quantity, with a little Christian culture smeared on like face cream.

To the average person, God is not a person to be cultivated; He is to be kept at arm's length. He is not considered a good neighbor, and He is very hard to please. Most people think of God as sort of a policeman, waiting around the corner to catch them in some wrongdoing. A little girl accidentally gave the average conception of God when she recited a Scripture verse and got it a bit confused. She said, "If God be for you, you are up against Him." That is the thinking of many people. If anyone is going to say that God is good, it will have to be His redeemed ones.

God is good. That is not an axiom; in other words, it is not a self-evident or universally recognized truth. It is a proposition; in other words, a plan suggested for acceptance; a proposition that is subject to proof. It is not a cliché. A cliché is a trite or overused expression or idea. Nor is it a slogan. A slogan is a catch phrase used in advertising or promotion. It is not propaganda. Propaganda is the systematic spread of a given doctrine or of allegations reflecting its views and interests. But it is true. God is good!

The devil is defeated, God is exalted, and Jesus is Lord! It's time for the redeemed to say so! It's time for the redeemed to stand up and speak up against drugs, crime, domestic violence, teen pregnancy, lack of discipline in the homes, homosexuality, sex-change operations, psychic hotlines, 900 numbers, and kids bringing guns to schools. In other words, the redeemed must speak up against sin! The redeemed of the Lord should say to a lost world that the Bible says that, "the wages of sin is death, but the gift of God is eternal life through Jesus Christ our Lord (Romans 6:23).

It's time for the redeemed of the Lord to say so!

The apostles, although they were persecuted, they still spoke the Word of God with boldness (Acts 4:29).

God does not have any coward soldiers in His army (Judges 7:3).

The Bible says, "If God be for you, who can be against you" (Romans 8:31)?

It's time for the redeemed to be like the apostles and Christians of the early Church, who turned the world upside down with the Gospel of Jesus Christ!

The redeemed of the Lord should take on one characteristic of the lion. The lion is called "the king of the beasts." Jesus is also referred to as "the Lion of the Tribe of Judah." The Bible says in Proverbs chapter 28 and verse 1 that the wicked fleeth when no man pursueth, but the righteous are bold as a lion!

It's time for the redeemed to go into the highways and the byways and the hedges and tell the world about Jesus! It's time for a change. It's time for the redeemed to be ignite by the fire of God's Word and burn bright as a torch in a dark world! It's time for the redeemed of the Lord to "say so!"

Don't let anyone fool you, but I'm here to tell you that:

God only has one Church; God only has one people! And these people are a born-again people; these people are a Spirit-filled people; these people are a Spirit-led people. These people are a "called out" people; they have been called out of sin. These people are a "called in" people. They have been called in to God's marvelous light. These people are a "called up" people; called up to live a higher lifestyle; called up to serve and live on a higher plane! These people are called to serve, worship, and live for the true and living God! These people are a "regenerated" people. These people, and only these people, are called "the redeemed of the Lord!"

In closing, it's time for "the redeemed of the Lord" to be like Queen Esther, who said, "If I perish, I perish, but I'm going to see the king!"

It's time for "the redeemed of the Lord" to be like David, who met the challenge of Goliath. David didn't back down from the enemy, but David met him face-to-face. David was anointed and redeemed of the Lord, and David let the enemy know who he was representing. David told Goliath, "You come to me with a sword, a shield, and a javelin, but I come to you in the name of the Lord! You have picked on and laughed at God's people long enough, and we are not going to take it anymore!"

You and I, as the redeemed of the Lord, have to draw the spiritual line in the sand and tell the enemy, "If you cross the line, it will be war!" And if he crosses the line, go forth with your spiritual armor on—the whole armor of God! And commence to put the enemy to flight, because the Lord is with you! And if God be for you, who can be against you? If you are the redeemed of the Lord today, I want you to stand up on your feet and give Him praise! Give Him praise! Give Him praise!

"It's time for the redeemed of the Lord to say so!"
"It's time for the redeemed of the Lord to say so!"
"It's time for the redeemed of the Lord to say so!"
"It's time for the redeemed to come out of the closets and tell the world that Jesus saves. Tell the world that Jesus heals. Tell the world that Jesus can deliver!
"It's time for the redeemed of the Lord to say so!"
"It's time for the redeemed of the Lord to say so!"

We must tell the world that it was not shining silver nor was it yellow gold that purchased our salvation, but it was the precious blood of Jesus! We must always remember that the Bible says that we were "bought with a price: therefore, glorify God in your body and in your spirit, which are God's" (1 Corinthians 6:20).

I don't know about you, but I'm glad that I am redeemed! I'm glad that I am redeemed! If you are here today and if you are redeemed, I challenge you to get up out of your seat and praise Him! Glorify Him! Worship Him! I challenge you in this challenge service to help me lift Jesus up! Help me give Him the glory! They say when praises go up, that blessings come down. Help me praise Him! I need the redeemed of the Lord to help me praise Him!

"It's time for the redeemed of the Lord to say so!"

"It's time for the redeemed of the Lord to say so!"

"It's time for the redeemed of the Lord to say so!"

Message #15

God's Detergent

Scriptural Text: Colossians 1:9-15

We see in our text that the apostle Paul is writing to the church at Colosse, although he never visited Colosse. Paul wrote this book from his prison cell. Now, Colosse was about one hundred miles east of Ephesus. It was a small town in the province of Asia. The church there may have been founded by Epaphras, who with many others, had probably been converted during Paul's three-year ministry in Ephesus. However, some false teachers at Colosse had undercut the major doctrines of Christianity, not the least of which was the Deity, Absolute Lordship, and sufficiency of Christ. Colossians sets forth Christ as Supreme Lord, in whose sufficiency the believers find completeness.

Let us focus on verse number 14. It says, "In whom we have redemption through His blood, even the forgiveness of sins." The title of this message is "God's Detergent."

Definition of detergent – A cleansing substance that has cleansing power. There are many types of detergents on the grocery store shelves today. Just walk in any grocery store in this country and you will find an aisle or a section that carries various types of detergents, such as liquids or powders or even tablets. The cost varies from product to product, depending on the brand name. Here are some detergent products that you might be familiar with and their claims to fame.

Shout – "Nothing gets out more tough stains better the first time."

Ultra Biz – "For fighting stains."
Dawn – "New fast-acting formula."
Ultra Ivory – "Now even milder on hands."
Ajax – "Tough on grease."
Ultra Palmolive – "Tough on grease, soft on hands."
Joy – "Improved formula."
Comet – "Bleaches tough stains."
Clorox Bleach – "Kills 99.9% of common household germs."
Formula 409 – "Improved grease-fighting formula."
Arm & Hammer – "Powers out dirt and odors."
Tide – "Deep-clean formula."
Gain – "Fresh wash."
Wisk – "Exceptional clean."
Surf – "Power fresh formula."
All – "Safely lifts tough stains."
Lysol – "Cuts grease and disinfects."
Fantastik – "Cuts grease, leaves no smeary residue."
Cheer – "New, improved formula, protects your clothing investment."

Some detergents cannot remove all stains because they are so tough to get out. You may have to repeat the washing process several times before your garments are cleaned. You may even have to take your clothes to the dry cleaners if the stains are still deeply imbedded. Sometimes the dry cleaners can easily remove those deeply imbedded stains and sometimes they cannot. In fact, sometimes it does more damage than good.

Some detergents need additives to help them in the cleaning process. For example, if you have white clothes with deeply imbedded stains, detergent alone in the wash may leave them dingy. But if you add bleach to the wash with your favorite detergent, your clothes will become whiter. Now when it comes to colored clothes, the former process for cleaning white clothes does not apply. And if you do apply bleach where it should not be applied, the results will prove disastrous.

God's Detergent

We have just been talking about the natural cleansing process for clothing. Now let's talk about *God's cleansing process* for a sin-stained soul.

Just as Shout claims "nothing gets out more tough stains better the first time," and Comet, which claims it "bleaches tough stains," or Dawn, which says it's "fast-acting," or Tide, that has a "deep-clean formula," I want you to know that God, the Heavenly Father, can cleanse a sin-stained soul like no man-made detergent can. You may ask, how can a sin-stained soul be cleansed? Well, I'm glad you asked! First...

God's detergent is cost effective because it's free! All it takes is your obedience to His Word. Come, with your sin-stained self, and let God's detergent wash you and make you clean. In the book of Isaiah, chapter 55 and verse 1, it says, "Ho, everyone that thirsteth, come to the waters, and he that hath no money, come, buy and eat; yea, come, buy wine and milk without money and without price."

Secondly, God's detergent can remove *all* of your sinful stains and make you clean. The Gospel of St. John, chapter 15 and verse 3 declares, "Now ye are clean through the word which I have spoken unto you."

Thirdly, God's detergent does not need any additives to clean you up! It is powerful enough all by itself. Therefore, He does not need any of our good works, social standing, political affiliations, or church denominations. The book of Hebrews, chapter 1 and verse 3 declares, "Who being the brightness of His glory, and the express image of His person, and upholding all things by the word of His power, when He had by Himself purged our sins, sat down on the right hand of the Majesty on high."

Lastly, God's detergent can cleanse any man's sin-stained soul, no matter what color you are, who you are, where you are, where you've been, or who you've been with. No matter how low or how high or no matter how deep you are in sin, God's detergent can still reach you even in your deep and difficult places. The Epistle of 1 John, chapter 1 and verse 7 declares, "But if we walk in the light, as He is in the light, we have fellowship one with another, and the blood of Jesus Christ, His Son, cleanses us from *all* sin."

Sin is a disease, a plague everyone is born into because of the first sin committed in the Garden of Eden by Adam and Eve. The book of Romans, chapter 3 and verse 23 declares, "For all have sinned and come short of the glory of God." Therefore, when we miss the glory of God, we miss the mark, the place where God wants us to be.

The book of James, chapter 4 and verse 17 declares, "Therefore, to him that knows to do good, and does it not, to him it is sin." We all have been drawn into situations and circumstances by the desires of our hearts; drawn into thoughts that we shouldn't think, conversations we shouldn't have, casting our focus on things we shouldn't focus on, and listening to things we shouldn't be listening to, as well as drawn into actions that we shouldn't engage in.

But God's detergent will wash away...

- Addictions
- Adultery
- Alcohol
- Being a busybody
- Cursing
- Fornication
- Gambling
- Greed
- Gossiping
- Hatred
- Illegal drug use
- Jealousy
- Killing
- Lusting
- Lying
- Misunderstandings
- Murmuring
- Negligence
- Pride
- Pornography
- Regrets
- Sickness

- Shame
- Stealing
- Sowing discord
- Tears
- Wickedness

God's detergent is...

- Our atoning blood
- Our banner of righteousness
- The chosen of the Father
- The diadem
- The express image of the Father
- The foundation of our faith
- The gift of God—freely given
- The hope of glory
- The inheritance
- Our justification
- The Kinsman Redeemer
- The Lamb of God who takes away our sins
- The Maker and Preserver of all things
- The Nazarene
- The olive tree
- The propitiation for our sins
- The Rose of Sharon
- The Son of the Highest
- The hidden treasure
- Urim and Thummin
- The Vine
- The Word of God
- Yeshua HaMashiach

Always remember, Jesus, who is God's detergent for a sin-stained soul, is the sinner's only hope. He was born of a virgin named Mary. He lived a sinless life, having been tested in all points, yet without sin; He suffered, bled, and died on the cross at Calvary. But to some people, this causes controversy. However, the Bible says, "And without controversy, great is the mystery of godliness: God was manifest in the flesh, justified in the Spirit, seen of angels, preached unto the Gentiles, believed on in the world, received up into glory (1 Timothy 3:16).

There's a hymn that comes to mind entitled, "There Is Power in the Blood," by Lewis E. Jones, who lived from 1865 to 1936, and these are the words:

Would you be free from the burden of sin?
There's power in the blood, power in the blood;
Would you o'er evil a victory win?
There's wonderful power in the blood.

There is power, power, wonder working power
In the blood of the Lamb;
There is power, power, wonder working power
In the precious blood of the Lamb.

There's another hymn that also comes to mind entitled, "Nothing But the Blood," by Robert Lowry, who was born in 1826 and died in 1899. These are the words:

What can wash away my sin?
Nothing but the blood of Jesus;
What can make me whole again?
Nothing but the blood of Jesus.

Oh! precious is the flow
That makes me white as snow;
No other fount I know,
Nothing but the blood of Jesus.

But wait...there's one more hymn that comes to mind and it is entitled, "There Is a Fountain," by William Cowper (pronounced Kooper), who lived from 1731 to 1800. These are the words:

There is a fountain filled with blood,

Drawn from Immanuel's veins,
And sinners plunged beneath that flood
Lose *all* their guilty stains.

Not a little bit, but they lose *all* their guilty stains!

On a personal note, having been out in the world and drawn far from the place where God wanted me to be, I'm glad that I heard about God's cleansing power, because then I understood that there was hope for even me. So I came and gave myself to the Lord, who cleansed and delivered me from my sins and gave me a new life. That's why I have a new walk, a new talk, a new mind, and a new heart to live for Jesus. That's why I can praise and bless His holy name!

Now if there's anyone here who needs God's cleansing power, it's available to you *right now!*

Message #16

God Is Still God

Scripture Text: Psalm 46:10

Amid life's uncertainties and the problems we face in the world today, we as Christians must make a decision to keep our trust and our faith in God and His Word. When things go wrong in life, what do we do and to whom do we turn? What is our stand? Do we throw in the towel and quit? Or do we press on in our Christian walk and remain faithful to God? These are questions that many don't want to deal with and that some refuse to face, because these issues involve maintaining faith in God through the hardships of life.

Problems, tests, trials, and disappointments in life are real facts, but a strong faith in God is the answer to every one of life's difficulties. We must realize that God has not promised us that we would never face a test or trial. But He has promised us that He would never leave us and that He would cause us to triumph, because He has overcome the world (St. John 16:33)!

The answer to life's problems is not to "hide our heads in the sand," hoping the problems will go away. Nor is the answer to question our faith in God. We must instead do as the Bible exhorts: "Trust in the Lord with all thine heart; and lean not unto thine own understanding" (Proverbs 3:5).

Many have faced adversity in life, yet they maintained their faith in God. If you were to talk to some of these people, you'd find that they are stalwart men and women of God today—not because of their adversity, but because they chose to persevere. With their eyes fixed on Jesus, they came through the storm and discovered once again the calm that awaited them on the other side.

The ocean of life may not always be as smooth as glass, but through faith in God, we always have an anchor of hope to steady us and keep us on course. So when the storms of life assail and everything appears to be going wrong, ask yourself, "Is not God still God? Or is He only God when things are going smoothly?" Purpose in your heart that the unchanging God is God at all times—when times are good and when times are difficult. In all places and under all circumstances, God is still God!

It's during the hard times that we need to dig our heels in the ground and make the decision, "I cannot be defeated, and I will not quit!" It's a decision that each of us has to make. We can allow the situations and circumstances of life to either bring us closer to God—to a place of confidence and certainty in Him—or drive us further away into the uncertainty and suffering of the world.

If you have been discouraged or have wavered in your faith, I encourage you to pick up the pieces of your disappointments and failures and make the decision to go on with God. Stand stronger on His Word than you ever have done before! Rise up to your full stature in Christ and be more determined than ever that victory belongs to you! The choice is yours. God is still God!

When I look at the sand, I know God is still God!

When I look at a tree, I know God is still God!

When I look at the oceans, the rivers, and the lakes, I know God is still God!

When I see the rain, I know God is still God!

When I see the lightning flashing across the sky, I know God is still God!

When I hear the thunder, I know God is still God!

When people don't understand me, I know God is still God!

When I'm treated unfairly, I know God is still God!

When I'm lied on and talked about, I know God is still God!

When I'm called everything but a child of God, I know God is still God!

When I'm backed up in a corner with no way out, I know God is still God!

So I'm here to encourage each one of you to always remember that God is still in control!

I'm glad that I know that God is still God!

On Monday—God is still God!

On Tuesday—God is still God!

On Wednesday—God is still God!

On Thursday—God is still God!

On Friday—God is still God!

On Saturday—God is still God!

On Sunday—God is still God!

Are you glad that God is still God? Well, help me praise Him! Praise Him! Praise Him!

Message #17

God Didn't Bring Us This Far to Leave Us

Scripture Text: 2 Samuel 7:18

In the Scripture lesson that was read to you today, we are going to focus on verse number 18. I will be reading it from the New King James translation, and it reads as follows:

> Then King David went in and sat before the Lord; and he said: "Who am I, O Lord God? And what is my house, that you have brought me this far? (NKJV)

And from this verse we will speak from the title: "God Didn't Bring Us This Far to Leave Us."

The Bible says that David "sat" before the Lord. Now "sat" as used in this passage of Scripture means, "remained." David spent a lengthy time before the Lord, that is, in the tent where the ark of the covenant stood.

In the beginning of this chapter, chapter 7 and verse 1, it tells us about a time when the Lord had given King David and his house (palace) rest from all of his enemies. In other words, the Lord gave David *peace*. David had captured the city of Jerusalem, and then he had captured the ark of the covenant. The ark represented the presence of the Lord, and the ark of covenant was in a tent.

David was living in a palace, and he felt bad because the ark was in a tent. He wanted to build a house for the Lord, but by him being a warrior, a man of war, a mighty man who had shed a lot of blood, God told David that his son, Solomon, would build the house for the Lord.

Now I want to go back and talk about *peace*. It is a beautiful thing to have peace: to have peace of mind; to have peace in the church; to have peace in the home; to have peace in the school system; to have peace in the workplace; to have peace from your supervisors; to have peace from your coworkers; to have peace from the criminal element in our neighborhoods, in our cities, in our state, and in our nation; to have peace from our government, and peace from our enemies.

The world thinks that they can find peace in a bottle of alcohol, or by taking drugs, or by other means of fleshly gratification. But we cannot experience real, true peace, until we allow the *Prince of Peace* to come into our hearts and set up His throne. I'm here to tell every one of us today that God didn't bring us this far to leave us. I'm going to tell you about four individuals who God didn't bring this far to leave them!

In the Word of God, it tells me of a young man named Joseph who was the son of Jacob by Rachel (Genesis 30:22-24). Joseph was loved by Jacob more than all his children because he was the son of his old age. Jacob made Joseph a coat of many colors. Joseph's brothers hated him and were jealous of him.

Joseph dreamed dreams and interpreted the meanings of them. He was sold into slavery by his brothers. They took his coat of many colors, covered it with animals' blood, and took it to their father and told him that Joseph was killed by an animal. Jacob's heart was broken, for he loved his son, Joseph, so very, very much. But God was still with Joseph through all of his trying times.

Joseph was lied on by Potiphar's wife and unjustly imprisoned in Egypt. While in prison he interpreted dreams for the butler and the baker, and was given favor by the captain of the guard. The Lord also gave Joseph favor with Pharaoh. Pharaoh was given a dream and no one in his kingdom was able to interpret his dream; but the Lord gave Joseph the interpretation of Pharaoh's dream. Pharaoh made Joseph the second most powerful man in Egypt.

Joseph prepared Egypt for famine, sold grains to his brothers, and then revealed his identity and reconciled with his brothers. Then Joseph sent for his father, Jacob. God didn't bring Joseph this far to leave him!

I know of another man in the Bible whose name was Moses. Moses led the children of Israel out of Egypt. He led them through the wilderness, toward the Promised Land. Pharaoh and his army began to pursue Moses and the children of Israel. Moses and the children of Israel got to the Red Sea, with the enemy coming behind them and mountains on either side of them.

The situation looked hopeless from the natural man's view, but I believe God said to Moses, "Moses, I didn't bring you this far to leave you," because Moses said to the children of Israel, "Do not be afraid. Stand still, and see the salvation of the Lord, which He will accomplish for you today. For the Egyptians, whom you see today, you shall see again no more forever."

Then Moses stretched out his hand over the sea and the Lord caused the sea to go back by a strong east wind all that night, and made the sea into dry land, and the waters were divided. And Moses stretched out his hand over the sea, and when the morning appeared, the sea returned to its full depth, while the Egyptians were fleeing into it. So the Lord overthrew the Egyptians in the midst of the sea. Then the waters returned and covered the chariots, the horsemen, and all the army of Pharaoh that came into the sea after them. Not so much as one of them remained.

But the children of Israel had walked on dry land in the midst of the sea and the waters were a wall to them on their right hand and on their left. So the Lord saved Israel that day out of the hand of the Egyptians, and Israel saw the Egyptians dead on the seashore. And Israel saw the great work which the Lord had done in Egypt; so the people feared the Lord, and believed the Lord and His servant, Moses (Exodus 14:13, 21, 27-31).

There is another man in the Bible. As a matter of fact, he is in our Scripture text. It's about David. David was the son of Jesse. David played the harp and tended his father's sheep. He was the youngest son of Jesse. The Lord was with David. The Lord delivered him from the paw of the lion and the paw of the bear, and he was given victory over both of them.

David slew the Philistine named Goliath. King Saul was jealous of David and wanted to kill him. King Saul had a son named Jonathan, whom David loved very much. They were very good friends. David was anointed king of Israel over all of his brothers.

David had a son named Solomon, whom God loved. God blessed Solomon to be the wisest and the wealthiest man on the earth. God didn't bring David that far to leave him! David's prayer of Thanksgiving (2 Samuel 7:18-29) is a prayer that is very humble.

In our text, David sat before the Lord, which means he remained a long time before the Lord. David asked the Lord a question, "Who *am* I, O Lord God? And what is my house, that You have brought me this far?" (NKJV). Have you ever thought about it? Who are we? I'll tell you who we are! We are the object of His love, because we are made in His image. If He loses man, He loses Himself. God loves you, because every time He sees you, He sees Himself.

In this great universe that we live in, God has five hundred million galaxies and four billion stars, and each one He has named. And yet He thinks about man. Who are we that the great God of creation thinks so highly of us? That's why the psalmist David said in Psalm 8:4-5:

> What is man, that thou art mindful of him? and the son of man, that thou visitest him? For thou hast made him a little lower than the angels, and hast crowned him with glory and honour.

God could have commanded man to exist by His spoken word, if He wanted to. But the awesome, all-powerful, all-knowing God took the time to form man with His own hands, from the dust of the ground. Not only did He form man with His hands, but He even took the time to breathe into man's nostrils the breath of life; and man became a living soul (Genesis 2:7). What a mighty God we serve! He really does care for us, because the Bible says that our God does not slumber, and He does not sleep (Psalm 121:4)! God didn't bring us this far to leave us!

Psalm 23:6 says, "Surely goodness and mercy shall follow me all the days of my life; and I shall dwell in the house of the Lord forever." The Bible says that God didn't bring us this far to leave us! As we walk along our Christian pathway, we may stumble and fall, but we have the divine escorts right there by our side—Goodness on one side and Mercy on the other side—to pick us up! God sees us through the eyes of faith! He sees us from "A" to "Z". He sees us as the finished products! He knows that we will end up at "Z", but in order to get to "Z" we have to go from the "Bs" to the "Ys" before we get to "Z"! We may have to go through the:

- **B** – Battles, bruises, bigotry.
- **C** – Conflicts, confusion, chaos.
- **D** – Disappointments, distresses, dangers, doubt, discouragements, difficulties.
- **E** – Envy, egos, emptiness.
- **F** – Frustrations, floods, fears.
- **G** – Guilt, greed, godlessness.
- **H** – Heartaches, headaches, hurts, humiliations, hatred.
- **I** – Irritations, injustices, insufficiency.
- **J** – Jealousy, judgments, jeers.
- **K** – Keepsakes, killjoys, knots.
- **L** – Loneliness, lusts, legalism.
- **M** – Mountains, materialism, moodiness.
- **N** – Negative, narrow-mindedness, neglectful.
- **O** – Offenses, oppositions, obstacles.
- **P** – Pitfalls, problems, pains, pressures.
- **Q** – Questions, quests, quitting.
- **R** – Rebukes, reprimands, rains.
- **S** – Sorrows, sadness, sin, sickness.
- **T** – Troubles, trials, temptations, tribulations, tragedies, tears.
- **U** – Unfit, unimportant, unrecognized.
- **V** – Vipers, valleys, volcanoes.
- **W** – Winds, waves, wonders.
- **X** – X-tremes, x-pressions, x-cuses.
- **Y** – Youthfulness, yokes, yielding.

But remember, although we may have to go through all of this... God didn't bring us this far to leave us! I said, "God didn't bring us this far to leave us!" He will bring you through from "B" to "Y" because He is God, and you are His child!

Remember I told you I was going to tell you about four individuals who God didn't bring this far to leave them? Well, I only told you about three. The fourth man was the same one that Daniel, the prophet, speaks about. King Nebuchadnezzar said to his counselors, "Lo, I see four men loose, walking in the midst of the fire, and they have no hurt; and the form of the fourth is like the Son of God (Daniel 3:25). And just in case you don't know who this fourth man is...His name is spelled J-E-S-U-S! J-E-S-U-S! J-E-S-U-S! Jesus is His name!

God didn't bring Jesus through forty-two generations, through all of the suffering, and through all of the agony, and to die that awful death on a cross to leave Him! God didn't bring His Son that far to leave Him! That's why on that third day morning, God raised Jesus from the grave! And when Jesus rose from the grave, having defeated death, hell, and the grave, and having the keys of all three, Jesus—not John, not Peter, not Paul—but Jesus was able to say, "All power is given unto Me in heaven and in earth!"

I'm glad that God didn't bring Jesus that far to leave Him, but God took Jesus all the way! Are you glad that God didn't bring us this far to leave us? He will take us all the way! Are you glad about it, Church? Are you really glad about it, Church? Well stand up on your feet and thank Him! Praise Him! Worship Him! Adore Him! Give Him praise! Give Him honor! Give Him glory! Shout, "Hallelujah!" Shout, "Thank You, Jesus!" Tell the Lord that you love Him! Tell the Lord that you love Him! God didn't bring us this far to leave us! Church, I said, "God didn't bring us this far to leave us!" Church, are you glad that God didn't bring us this far to leave us? I'm glad! I'm glad! I'm glad!

Some of you are so dignified that you have forgotten how to praise the Lord!

Some of you are too cute to praise the Lord!

Some of you have gotten so rich that you have forgotten where God has brought you from!

Some of you are so holy that you can't even shake your brother and sister's hand!

But I don't ever want to forget what the Lord has done for me! I don't ever want to forget where the Lord has brought me from! Can I get a witness? Somebody say, "Yes!" Say, "Yes!" Say, "Yes!"

So remember today that whether you are going up the mountain or going through the valley, as long as God is leading you, be assured that everything is going to be all right!

No matter what you are going through, just remember that God is in control. God is in charge. He has brought you up until this present hour, and no matter how it may look, no matter how bad the storm is, no matter how hard the rain is falling, no matter how hard the wind is blowing, I just want all of us to remember that, "God didn't bring us this far to leave us!"

Give Him praise! Give Him praise! Give Him praise!

God didn't bring us this far to leave us! He is everything we need!

He is our provider, for He will make a way out of no way! He will provide!

He is our battle-ax. If you trust Him, He will fight for you!

He is our shepherd. He will lead us and guide us into all truth and righteousness!

He is our bright sunshine in the morning!

He is our bright sunshine in the noonday!

He is our bright sunshine until the end of the day, and then at night He is our bright and morning star!

He is our counselor, for He will always give you the right counsel!

He is our lawyer, for He has never, ever lost a case!

He is our strong tower, for He will protect us from the enemy!

He is our stronghold buster, for He will pull down the strongholds of the enemy in our lives!

He is our intercessor. He will pray or intercede on our behalf to the Father!

He is the Anointed One, for He is our burden-removing, yoke-destroying power of God!

God didn't bring us this far to leave us! I said, "God didn't bring us this far to leave us!" I don't know about you, but I'm glad! I'm glad! I'm glad! If you are glad that God didn't bring you this far to leave you, I want you to stand up on your feet and give God some praise! Give Him some praise! Give God some praise!

Church, I don't know about you, but I'm glad that God didn't bring me this far to leave me! How about the rest of you? Are you all glad that God didn't bring you this far to leave you? Can I get somebody to testify that God didn't bring them this far to leave them?

Choir: Can you testify that God didn't bring you this far to leave you?

Musicians: Can you testify that God didn't bring you this far to leave you?

Preachers: Can you testify that God didn't bring you this far to leave you?

Deacons: Can you testify that God didn't bring you this far to leave you?

Deaconesses: Can you testify that God didn't bring you this far to leave you?

Ushers: Can you testify that God didn't bring you this far to leave you?

Congregation: Can you testify that God didn't bring you this far to leave you?

Can I get somebody to help me praise this awesome God that we serve? Stand up on your feet and praise Him! Praise Him! Praise Him!

www.ingramcontent.com/pod-product-compliance
Ingram Content Group UK Ltd.
Pitfield, Milton Keynes, MK11 3LW, UK
UKHW041954230426
12048UKWH00008B/331